CW00409647

THE STORY OF THE
WELLCOME
TRUST

Dedication

To Billie who was my companion and partner during all the years described in this book and to our daughters Judy and Sherry and their families.

To give away money is an easy matter, and in any man's power. But to decide to whom to give it and how large and when, and for what purpose and how is neither in any man's power – nor an easy matter.

Aristotle

THE STORY OF THE
WELLCOME
TRUST

Unlocking Sir Henry's legacy to medical research

Peter Williams

Publisher's note

To make it easier for the reader, the biographies and certain other quoted matter have been printed over a light grey tint.

First published 2010 by

JJG Publishing
Sparrow Hall
Hindrigham
Norfolk NR21 0DP

Copyright © 2010 Peter O Williams

ISBN 978-1-899163-92-2

No part of this work may be reproduced in any form and by any means without prior written permission of the author or publisher.

Designed by Graham Hiles

Printed in China through Colorcraft Ltd., Hong Kong

CONTENTS

FOREWORD

By Sir Stanley Peart, Wellcome Trustee 1975-92, and
Sir Roger Gibbs, Trustee 1983-99, Chairman 1989-99

Stanley Peart writes

When Sir Henry Dale invited me to his office to explain the findings of
my research I was naturally honoured but unaware of his association with
the Wellcome Trust. Years later after serving on the Medical Research
Council I was agreeably surprised when Peter Williams aroused my interest
in succeeding Sir John McMichael as a trustee as I had long admired his
achievements. I respected my fellow trustees for their scientific strengths
and the possibility of supporting research in a practical fashion attracted
me. Lord Franks was the chairman and Peter Williams the director. Peter
had the difficult task of marrying the trustees aims with that of the
chairman, while ensuring that his own view of the needs of the scientific
community, gleaned from his own contacts and that of his admirable team,
engaged in continuous field work out of the office, were properly met. I
soon realised that the Trust income depended on the fiercely guarded link
between Franks and the company chairman, Shepperd, and that the
trustees requests for more income were discouraged. All this was to change
in an explosive fashion when David Steel, former chairman of BP,
succeeded Franks and asked the simple question. "As the Trust owns the
Company why can we not get more financial support from it?" He carried
the trustees with him and imposed his view on the reluctant company
managers, both here and in the United States.

Roger Gibbs takes up the story

When David Steel joined the Trust in 1981, its assets had an estimated
value of £250 million. By the end of 1999, the Trust's portfolio had a
market value of over £14 billion, making it the largest grant giving charity
in the world. This extraordinary financial success was in no small measure
due to David Steel. It was he who set the Trust on the right financial course
by taking its 100% owned pharmaceutical company, The Wellcome
Foundation Limited, public in 1986. We, his successors, took his
diversification policy through to completion. This exciting, indeed

vii

remarkable investment story is told most interestingly by Neil Collins in Chapter 11 of this fascinating book by Peter Williams.

The success of the Wellcome Trust is due to so many different individuals, scientific and lay. For me it was also of over-riding importance that it was always the greatest fun to work there, not least in the days of Peter Williams, an outstanding communicator and formidable director.

PREFACE

In 1986 Professor Rupert Hall and Dr Ben Bembridge wrote a history of the Wellcome Trust published with the title *Physic and Philanthropy*. On the dedication page they quote a letter written on September 20th 1943 by Sir Henry Dale, chairman of the Trust, to Professor Elliot, another trustee, which reads, 'I am wondering whether our experience as trustees will eventually be more suitable for record as a novel or a play.' I think he was referring to the extraordinary matters they had had to deal with – things that they would have never anticipated when they accepted the appointments.

Physic and Philanthropy is neither a novel nor a play but a very detailed account of the first 50 years of the Trust and therefore not addressed to someone wishing to get an easily digestible understanding of the whole story. I have decided to write this up with a more personal broad brush approach. Hopefully, it is indeed 'The unlocking of Sir Henrys legacy to medical research'. The memoir of the early years illustrates that the people involved in the evolution were human and what occurred depended on the characters of the trustees and the staff. However, what I have written can only be my view. If some of my criticisms cause any offence to the families of these characters I apologise. Evolution is not pre-thought and no one is perfect.

The story runs from the birth in 1853 of a boy in a remote area of Minnesota, through the creation of one of the wealthiest private sources of funds in the world for the support of medical research to its manifestation today.

My qualification for attempting this task is that I worked for the Trust from 1960 to 1991, the last 26 years as its director and chief executive. During this time the Trust's annual disbursements rose from £1 million to £100 million when I retired. Today it is about £600 million. It was my main task to create and manage the way in which the Trust's income was used for the purposes stipulated in Sir Henry Wellcome's will. The story goes up to my retirement for the overall picture but is extended to 1995 by Sir Roger Gibbs who led the 1992 worldwide share sale of almost 35% of the

Wellcome Company and the sale of the remaining 39.6% to Glaxo in February 1995 and so, by 2000 created a capital base of £15billion for the Trust's operations. The story since 1995 has not been published as a book but can be read from its annual reports up to 2009. These are available on the internet.

The story is mainly written from memory or facts gleaned from Rupert Hall's book and Roy Church and Tilli Tansey's book about the Company up to 1936 when Wellcome died, a biography of Henry Wellcome written by Henry Rhodes James and a booklet *In Pursuit of Excellence* published by the Wellcome Foundation at its centenary in 1980. In addition I interviewed the main personalities involved in the story and I have drawn on this material.

As director of the Trust I knew all the people concerned in every aspect of its evolution. Three of the original board of five trustees were still in post when I arrived. Sir Henry Dale, aged 85, resigned soon after but kept an office and continued to attend meetings for the next three years. He was succeeded by Lord Piercy who was in post for five years. Lord Franks, Sir David Steel and Sir Roger Gibbs followed in turn during my directorship. All of the trustees became my close associates and many my personal friends. This was also true of my colleagues who continue to keep in touch with me in retirement.

The story encompasses the growth of a pharmaceutical company from its origins to its near bankruptcy after the Second World War and then to becoming an immensely profitable enterprise based on the research of its scientists, particularly in its laboratories in North America.

The latter part is about how a Trust set up and implemented a policy to support medical research and medical history using the dividends from the Company which it owned. This is a tale about the way in which the trustees of a Will and the staff they employed made the progress described. No one person could have had the skills for all these tasks and the way in which it proceeded had many interesting features. For instance an aspect of the story not central to the theme of medical research in industry and the universities is the support of medical history. Sir Henry Wellcome collected an immense library and museum on the history of mankind and when he died he left it to his trustees to turn his collections into an usable entity that could be seen and studied by scholars and other interested people. The arrangements that were made to this end are a story in itself. Finally there is the detail of how a privately owned business was sold so as to realise an immense fortune to carry out the charitable purposes set out in Sir Henry Wellcome's will. The story provides an insight into industry, university research and the financial world and how these worked together based on Britain and America to the benefit of many parts of the world including the tropics.

The short biographies are about some of the people who were part of the history of the Trust and are reproduced to expand the background without disturbing the flow of the story.

THE CHRONOLOGY OF THE WELLCOME TRUST AND WELLCOME FOUNDATION

1853	Henry Solomon Wellcome born; 1865 Wellcome leaves school
1886–1878	Wellcome works in pharmacies in Rochester, Chicago and Philadelphia; 1878 Wellcome licensed as a pharmacist at the Philadelphia College of Pharmacy
1880	Burroughs and Wellcome form a partnership in London (BW)
1884	Trade name *Tabloid* first used
1888	Factory opened in Dartford on a ten year lease with option to buy
1895	Burroughs dies. First batch of diphtheria antiserum produced from horses
1901	Wellcome marries Syrie Barnardo
1904	Wellcome visits Khartoum and funds tropical laboratories in the Gordon Memorial College. Starts his archaeological interests. Physiological Research Laboratories opened in London
1905	Wellcome transfers responsibility for Business to Pearson
1906	Wellcome Chemical Laboratories opened
1907	BW USA established in New York. Nevin as President
1913	Balfour returns to London from Khartoum and is made director of Wellcome Bureau of Scientific Research and starts Museum of Medical Science
1914–1918	World War 1
1923	Balfour moves to London School of Hygiene and Tropical Medicine, Kellaway is made director of research
1924	Wellcome Foundation Ltd is incorporated

1925	BW USA moves to Tuckahoe, New York
1927	Diphtheria vaccine (TAF) is made and marketed
1932	Wellcome signs his Will
1934	Wellcome Building opened
1936	Wellcome dies aged 83. Wellcome Trust created. Dale awarded Nobel Prize
1937	Lyall dies and Dale becomes chairman of Trust
1939	World War 2 commences
1940	Wellcome Foundation head office moves to Wellcome Building after Snow Hill office destroyed in bombing. Pearson has his appointment ended by trustees. Bennett replaces him
1942	Hitchings appointed head of biochemical research at USA Company
1944	Trudy Elion joins Hitchings
1945	Bennett's appointment terminated and Sier takes charge. Nevin retires from USA Co and Bill Creasy takes his place as President
1947	Marzine marketed
1952	Glenny awarded Jenner medal for his research on diphtheria
1953	Michael Perrin succeeds Sier as chairman of Foundation. Adamson becomes research director
1955	John Boyd becomes a trustee, Burroughs Wellcome Fund established in the USA
1957–1966	Trust's main support provided for university buildings and equipment
1958	Trust's office moves to 52 Queen Anne Street
1960	Dale retires from Trust and becomes Chief Scientific Adviser. Piercy succeeds Dale, John McMichael becomes a trustee, Williams appointed Assistant Scientific Secretary. Museum and library sold to the Trust.
1963	Williams become Scientific Secretary in succession to Frank Green

1964	Boyd retires from trusteeship
1965	Lord Franks chairman of Trust, Edda Hanington joins Trust, Williams Secretary as well as Scientific Sec, Director 2 years later.
1966	Fred Coe appointed President Burroughs Wellcome USA
1966	Policy statement published by Trust. Zyloric marketed by Company
1967	History of Medicine Panel appointed
1968	Septrin and Imuran marketed
1970	Perrin retires, Gray takes over, Factory in USA moves to N. Carolina
1970, 71, 76, 77	Company wins awards for export achievement
1971	Headquarters of BW USA moves to North Carolina
1972	Trust moves to Park Square West; History of Medicine Units launched in Oxford and Cambridge
1973	Poynter retires from History Institute
1976	Museum of the History of Medicine put on permanent loan to the Science Museum
1977	Shepperd succeeds Gray as chairman of Company
1980	Wellcome Foundation Limited 100 years old; *In Pursuit of Excellence* published
1982	Sir David Steel becomes chairman of the Trust in succession to Franks
1985	Trust 50 years old Her Majesty the Queen and the Duke of Edinburgh attend soirée at Wellcome Building; *Physic and Philanthropy* published 1986 Wellcome Foundation Limited goes public as Wellcome PLC 1988 Hitchings and Elion win Nobel Prize 1989; Foundation moves out of Wellcome Building; 1990 Steel retires and Roger Gibbs becomes chairman
1991	Williams retires; Bridget Ogilvie appointed director
1992	Second share sale, worldwide. Trust moves to Wellcome Building
1994	Sale of Company to Glaxo
1997	Meeting at the Burroughs Wellcome Fund

1999	Sir Roger Gibbs retires as chairman of Trust
2000	Draft of sequence of human genome published
2003	Mike Dexter retires and Mark Walport succeeds him as director
2004	Strategic awards, Stem Cell Research Centre, Cambridge. Neuro - imaging of the brain initiated
2005	Strategic plan 2005-2010 published. Sanger Institute extended
2006	Biobank project launched
2007	Sir William Castell appointed chairman in succession to Sir Dominic Cadbury
2008	Wellcome Collection exhibition opened

ACKNOWLEDGEMENTS

This book came to be written because Sir Peter Cazalet a former Wellcome trustee, invited Sir Stanley Peart, Sir Roger Gibbs and me to lunch in December 2007. Not surprisingly the conversation turned on our days at the Wellcome Trust. We all felt that we had been participants in a fascinating chain of events and that it ought to be written up. It might have stopped there but I was at a loose end and had been stimulated to do something about it. I did not contemplate writing it myself as I felt that the deterioration of my short term memory would make the task impossible. So I set about looking for a ghost writer. My daughter made some enquiries which eventuated in Roddy Bloomfield and Jeremy Greenwood coming to see me. When I told them the story Jeremy said he had someone in mind as a ghost writer. I supposed at this stage that the Trust might like to have the story written but they did not offer to fund the project. I told Jeremy and he said that he thought I could write it and that he would help me. In some trepidation I took up his offer.

Roger, Stan and I met and I enlisted their support because I could not deal with the sales of the Wellcome shares and I needed Stan's critical scientific overview.

At the suggestion of Christopher Fildes, Roger asked Neil Collins to write a chapter about the sales. Philip Bradley assessed the Company's financial reports before the first sale began. The book gradually came together during 2008 and early 2009. I could not have undertaken the task without the painstaking support of Jeremy Greenwood.

My other acknowledgement goes to my son-in-law Dr Martin Ford whose knowledge of the pharmaceutical industry was important for writing the chapters about the business of the Wellcome Company and his skill with using computers made it possible for me to keep my head above water as he organised the book into a sensible shape to take to the publishers.

I could not have written this book without all this help. I was also right about the problem of short term memory in writing a book when you are in your eighties; you tend not to register repetitions as you read the proof so I apologise to readers for any that I have not noticed!

CHAPTER 1

Sir Henry Wellcome

Henry Solomon Wellcome was born in Wisconsin, USA, in 1853. In his early childhood his father, a small farmer and minister of religion, moved westward with his family into the neighbouring state of Minnesota, then so near to the frontier of American civilisation that they were to become involved in defensive warfare against an attack by the Sioux Indian tribe. They settled in a locality named Garden City, Blue Earth County, about 100 miles to the south of Rochester, Minnesota. Garden City thus became for Henry the centre of his boyhood memories and the object of his most important personal bequests. It was a deeply religious household as his father was an Adventist preacher who was often away from home spreading the word. They were not well off. Henry was a boy with a good but not outstanding intelligence. He enjoyed the friendships provided by the community and was a keen canoeist and could handle a gun. He attended the community school which had been opened in a log-cabin in 1854 and had 58 pupils. It was very cold in winter but the teacher rose above that to give the boys a good basic education and no less than ten of Henry's contemporaries went on to have very successful careers. He left school at 13 and went to work for his uncle Jacob who was a medical doctor in practice in Garden City. He ran his own pharmacy above his surgery. His uncle urged him to go to College to study medicine but Henry was more attracted to pharmacy.

A few years later Henry became an assistant in a local pharmacy in Rochester, where he attracted the attention of Dr William Mayo, father of the surgeons William and Charles who were to make that city famous as the home of the Mayo Clinic and Foundation. Dr Mayo senior encouraged

1

Henry to become qualified in pharmacy and so a few years later he moved to Chicago to work in a pharmacy and then to Philadelphia where he was able to enrol in the College of Pharmacy and get trained in evening classes in the winter. After two years he passed the tests and graduated so that he had a licence to practise. It was in Philadelphia that he first met his future partner Silas Mainville Burroughs, a fellow student who was seven years his senior and had considerably more experience.

Henry then joined the New York firm McKesson and Robbins as one of their sales representatives and as such travelled widely in North and South America. In Peru and Ecuador he made a study of the cultivation of the Cinchona trees and maybe this experience caused the earliest stirrings of his interest in the history of medicine.

In 1880 Henry travelled to London, at the invitation of Burroughs but still as a representative of McKesson and Robbins. Wellcome heard from him that he had set up a company in 1878 to develop his own ideas and accepted his offer of partnership. Burroughs, who was representing other American pharmaceutical interests, had seized on the opportunity of developing a British market for a range of medicaments presented with accurate dosage, in the form of compressed tablets which were replacing the old fashioned pills, draughts and powders in the USA. He saw in Wellcome a perfect counterpart to run the administration of the Company in London while he went off to sell its medicines all over the world. At first the new business was essentially an importing agency for American products; but the rapid expansion of the UK market soon made it necessary to manufacture in England and factories were opened in Wandsworth (1880) and later Dartford (1888).

In 1884 Wellcome invented the word "Tabloid" and registered it as a trademark on behalf of Burroughs Wellcome. The name caught the public imagination and played a large part in the success of the business. In fact it caught on to such an extent that, in 1904, Wellcome had to establish his proprietary right to protect his trademark from competing pharmaceutical companies.

Meanwhile the partners had begun to find their views divergent on the conduct of the business and its future development. It had become apparent that the partnership would not survive. However in 1895 Burroughs died of pneumonia when on holiday in France and as a consequence Wellcome became the sole proprietor of the business.

Henry Wellcome established his position as the supreme Director and retained for himself the right to criticise and even countermand the decisions of his subordinates. Nothing could be settled without his signature, so important decisions on policy might be delayed while he was abroad – an old fashioned management style which was to haunt the Company as it expanded.

Wellcome was a man of attractive personal qualities and his complex character had strands of generous enterprise, perfectionist idealism and even a missionary zeal. These traits attracted loyal staff of character and ability to his service and enabled them to tolerate his autocracy. His genial gift of hospitality led him to have a wide circle of interesting friends and he became a leader of the American community in London. For instance he met Henry Morton Stanley on his way through London on his expedition to find David Livingstone in Africa and gave him six portable medicine chests. This gift and others to later explorers, Byrd, Shackleton, Nansen, Scott and Theodore Roosevelt, attracted much publicity and made his name a household word. Following Stanley's African expeditions inspired him to become interested in the diseases of the tropics and the attitude of primitive people to disease. These and other factors made him even more interested in the history of medicine and widened the range of his collections into ethnology.

Wellcome was perhaps the first to recognise the need for a research organisation in a company which could plan its programmes independently but make a contribution to the pharmaceutical business. He must have recognised that immunological remedies would need to have a continuous association with research as a condition of efficient and progressive production. His earliest research department, although called the Wellcome Physiological Research Laboratories, founded in 1894, was for its first ten years almost fully engaged in the production of diphtheria antitoxin. Nevertheless he regarded these laboratories and the Chemical Research Laboratories (1896) as a private and personal enterprise.

In 1904, while convalescing in Khartoum after a serious bout of pneumonia, he developed a close friendship with Lord Kitchener and this led to his building and endowing the Wellcome Tropical Laboratories in the Gordon Memorial College there. A fuller account of the Sudan operation is given in chapter 7.

In 1905 Henry Wellcome decided to delegate responsibility for the Company to George Pearson, so that he could spend most of his time travelling in pursuit of his collecting hobby while taking a personal interest in the activities of the research workers in his laboratories. It was convenient for these key people to be on the Company's payroll but not under its direction. Wellcome continued to insist on being involved in the major decisions. He was no longer enthusiastic about the development of the business and so it did not receive the positive drive that he had given it when he was in daily contact. He does not appear to have been bothered as to where the Company was going as long as he received his salary as Governing Director and a handsome dividend for him to spend on his collecting. The Company continued to make good profits but it was not progressing with the times, so essential for a viable business.

Wellcome was living a new life. He had married in 1901 and was enjoying himself unhampered by the daily demands of the business. His new wife, Syrie, was the daughter of Dr Barnardo, who had founded Barnardo's Homes for orphan children. She was much younger than Wellcome, now 48, who had lived the life of a bachelor for many years. He continued to pursue his interests and so instead of a stately house in the London area she found herself always travelling while he indulged his hobby. She was not interested in his collections and soon became bored. They had a child, Mountney, who was found in due course not to be up to playing a part in the business and eventually, during a visit to Ecuador, while he was undertaking a study of the health problems encountered in the construction of the Panama Canal, they had a bust up when he accused her of being unfaithful and she went back to England with Mountney. They never spoke again and the marriage was dissolved in 1916 when Syrie had a child fathered by Somerset Maugham who she subsequently married – once more very unhappily.

In 1924 Henry Wellcome registered a limited liability company called the Wellcome Foundation Limited with a notional capital of one million £1 shares, all held by himself. This new company included the world-wide pharmaceutical business, all his laboratories and all of his collections. There could be no doubt now that all Wellcome's activities were strictly regarded by him as part of the business.

In 1932 he signed his will which would, when he died, turn over to his trustees the management of all his assets. The board of trustees became known as the Wellcome Trust.

Henry Wellcome became a British citizen in 1910 and was knighted in 1932 as a generous supporter of medical research. He became a Fellow of the Royal Society as 'one who has rendered conspicuous service to the cause of science' and died peacefully in the London Clinic on 23 July 1936.

The urn with Sir Henry's ashes was placed in the bookcase of the director of the Wellcome Museum. When I took over that office I found it and decided that it should have a more appropriate resting place. Arrangements were made for the ashes to be buried in the churchyard of St Paul's Cathedral and, on 18 February 1987, a service was held in the Crypt to honour the memory of Sir Henry Wellcome. A plaque was placed on the wall of the crypt.

CHAPTER 2

Sir Henry Wellcome's Will and the First Thirty Years of the Wellcome Trust

The will of Sir Henry Wellcome was long and complicated but could be summarised as follows

1 The Foundation should be run by Mr George Pearson and a Board of Directors.

2 The laboratories should continue with their independent programmes.

3 The historical collections should be sorted and catalogued and exhibited to the public.

4 The dividends of the Company should be used as a charity to support medical research and medical history. (Unfortunately Wellcome had not created a charity during his lifetime which meant that the death duties were much larger than they might have been – £2 million leaving just £1.1 million.)

5 The Company should not be sold unless there proved to be an unavoidable reason.

6 The trustees of his will were to carry out his wishes but leave the Company to manage the affairs of the Foundation (i.e. everything). So the trustees had no power to carry out the purposes of the will if Pearson did not produce the funds or allow access to the laboratories or the collections.

The will made no stipulation about the age at which trustees should retire. As a consequence the board of trustees were all over the age of 70 and several over 80 when Henry Dale retired at the age of 85. Lord Piercy, who succeeded Dale as chairman, was 74 and went on for 5 years until he was 79. After that a retirement age of 70 was agreed by the trustees and 67 for scientific members.

The will was signed in 1932 – four years before Henry died. To understand why it described his wishes in such a clumsy way as to cause his trustees considerable difficulties one has to realise that he was 79 years old and was simply asking them to take over where he had left off. The lawyers who had drafted the will were trustees, Lyall and Bullock, and so must take some responsibility for the failure to create a charity and the lack of realisation that the structure used by Wellcome during his lifetime and now delegated to his trustees to manage his laboratories and collections, could not work once he had died.

He had divided his life's interests into two sections: the pharmaceutical company which earned the money and which he had left to be managed by Pearson for the past 30 years, and the history of medicine and the research laboratories. For convenience he had left the Company to administer the finances and employment of the staff of the laboratories and the historical museums and library.

The first board of trustees, formed in 1936, consisted of the two lawyers, Lyall and Bullock; an accountant, Martin Price; and two medical scientists, Dale and Elliott. Dale said that some of them were not aware that they had been selected! The lawyers who drafted the will at least must have known that they were on the list. They all accepted but in the case of the scientists they had first to ascertain that their connection to a pharmaceutical company would not be in conflict with their positions as Director of the National Institute of Medical Research (Dale) and Professor of Medicine at University College London (Elliot). Lyall died in 1937 and as he was not replaced for some years the board was two scientists a lawyer and an accountant. Sir Henry Dale became Chairman and continued in that role until 1960 when he resigned and became Chief Scientific Adviser.

The invitation to serve as a trustee must have been very attractive, especially to the scientists who saw their role as the provision of support to medical research – an activity that had dominated their lives and in which they, especially Dale who had won a Nobel Prize in 1936, had attained greatness.

The trustees of Wellcome's will were therefore required to look after his empire but could not do anything about the historical collections or the research laboratories because they were under the direction of George Pearson who maintained this position in opposition to the trustees even though he had no knowledge of either subject field. When Martin Price, the accountant trustee, examined the affairs of the Company he revealed how it had been gradually running down since 1929. The overall situation came to a head in April 1940 at a joint meeting of the board of trustees and the board of directors when they all agreed that Pearson had to go.

This did not, however, resolve the problem because death duties had to be paid and during the war taxation absorbed all profits. Mr TRG Bennett who had taken over from Pearson tried to revive the business after the war but made a number of unwise decisions which resulted in the Company degenerating by 1945 to near bankruptcy – only prevented by a large bank loan and the transfer of funds from the American branch.

The situation of the Company was reviewed by an accountant Mr HE Sier at the request of Martin Price, and the deficiencies were considered to be so damaging that Mr Bennett the chairman was forced to resign. Sier became chairman in 1948 and by using sound management brought the company back into balance. When he had reached the retirement age in 1953, Michael Perrin, who had experience of science in industry from working at ICI and on the Atomic Energy project during the war, was appointed by the trustees to succeed him. The trustees believed that the chairman should have an understanding of science in industry. This was contrary to the view of Sier and Denis Wheeler, the managing- director, who believed that financial experience was the key to good management. The board of trustees was led by Sir Henry Dale and he could not forget that Pearson and Bennett, who were not scientists, had brought it to its knees. The recovery created by Sier and Wheeler did not convince him that that was the way to go so Michael Perrin became chairman and Denis Wheeler was appointed joint managing-director with C G Oakes from the Australian company.

This difference in view between the trustees and the Company was to persist for the rest of the era when the Company was beholden to the Trust for the appointment of its chairman. This was certainly Sir Stanley Peart's view when Alfred Shepperd, the director of finance, was appointed chairman but the trustees bowed to the opinion of Franks who was then very dominant as chairman of the Trust. Up to about 1950 it was impossible to carry out the philanthropic purposes of Wellcome's will as the Company was not making a profit and in consequence the historical collections had to wait to be sorted and catalogued and there were no funds to distribute to support medical research and medical history.

There was however one bright spot on the horizon. The Company's subsidiary in America, unaffected by the war, was turning in a very rich profit, mainly from the sales of a tabloid aspirin compound, Empirin. The USA Company was virtually an independent entity with its own board and a go-ahead President who was not afraid to challenge the board in England

The other cause for hope was that the American Company had set up a research laboratory of its own sanctioned by Wellcome but contrary to the wishes of Pearson. In 1942 the laboratory had recruited the brilliant George Hitchings to lead its biochemistry department and he started a research programme that soon began to promise future products. Obviously if this came to fruition there was a chance that the whole Company would become profitable again and begin to yield funds for the philanthropic activities of the Trust. The income of the Company earned in America was, quite rightly, freely spent in supporting Hitchings in every way possible.

During these developments at the Foundation, Dale had remained steadfast as chairman of the Trust. When Lord Piercy took over his main concern was, as can be imagined, with methods for raising funds to finance the development of the Company. By 1965 an income of about £1 million per annum was becoming available to the trustees and these funds were mainly given to the universities to build laboratories and purchase major items of equipment – but otherwise Piercy's five years as chairman did not mark any particular changes in the fortunes of the Trust.

Dale was still very active as chief scientific adviser and in 1955 Sir John Boyd had become a trustee. Both had had a close association with the laboratories established by Wellcome before the war and had resisted all Perrin's attempts to change them from academic research to a programme that would benefit the Company, so well exemplified by Hitchings in the USA.

Professor John (later Sir John) McMichael, the director of the Postgraduate Medical School, had succeeded Dale as a trustee in 1960 and he brought a modern outlook to the research supported by the trustees.

Thus concluded the first 29 very difficult years, but by 1965 the situation had stabilized and as I entered the scene the two organisations were poised to develop with exciting momentum.

Sir Henry Dale

Sir Henry Dale was 84 when I first met him. In his time he was probably Britain's greatest scientist in the bio-medical field. He had been President of the Royal Society during the war and had won the Nobel Prize for physiology in 1936 for his work on neuro-humoral transmission.

At the age of 84 he still had an enormous knowledge of the current state of research in the biological sciences and a great contact with the leaders of the medico-scientific world. He was naturally given to a considerable amount of reminiscence in his conversation – much of it about the earlier work in which he had participated. He had been a trustee for 24 years and during most of that time had run the activities of the Trust with the assistance of his secretary, although the secretaryship and financial affairs of the board of trustees were undertaken by Mr Jack Clarke. There had not been major funds to distribute then and so his main concern had been to establish the charitable organization that could look after the investments of the Trust (largely the ownership of the Wellcome Foundation Limited) and be ready to disburse funds when dividends began to flow from the Company. When I first came to the Trust Dale was the ultimate decision maker on anything scientific to do with the Trust. He, together with John Boyd, Frank Green and me met about once a week to discuss matters of significance that had come through the post, as well as considering travel grant applications. The meetings were somewhat lengthy and tedious considering the limited amount of business that they conducted.

Dale became the Chief Scientific Adviser and retained his office in the Trust. Effectively, very little had changed since Dale continued to wish to overlook everything that happened and, as Chief Scientific Adviser, he chaired the Scientific Committee which now had added to it Professor John McMichael. For about four years this comprised the scientific assessment machinery of the Trust. He also sat on the right hand of Lord Piercy, at the trustees' meetings and intervened frequently to block changes. Piercy said to me shortly before he retired that he had found it impossible to be innovative as long as Dale was there without offending the "old man".

When he retired with Lady Dale, who by this time was completely blind, to a nursing home in Cambridge he continued to receive the papers of the Trust and Dr Edda Hanington and I used to visit him once a month during which visits he would tell us what decisions should be made on the applications going before the trustees. His last intervention was when we visited him two days before he died.

Dale's devotion to the initial years of the Trust was enormous.

Sir John Boyd

Sir John Boyd succeeded Professor Elliott as a trustee in 1955. Henry Dale knew him well because of his war record and his appointment as director of the Wellcome Laboratory of Tropical Medicine after the war. Sir John was a very eminent figure in tropical medicine, served on all the committees of that subject, and had been President of the Royal Society of Tropical Medicine & Hygiene and was knighted for his services in its Jubilee Year. His research had been in the field of the bacteria that cause dysentery and he was, in 1960, still working on the phage system, viruses of bacteria, in a laboratory provided for him in the Wellcome Building. Sir John's role at the Trust was to concern himself with its tropical interests. He was a very pleasant person but with the Scottish tendency to be rather reserved and only to accept the views of people of mature age. Nevertheless, I remember two extremely enjoyable overseas visits with him. The one to Denmark in connection with the Carlsberg-Wellcome Fellowships, and the other to Jamaica, following on a request from John Waterlow that we might create rather more long-standing funding for research in Jamaica. In the Jamaican case he was reluctant to commit the Trust to any long-term activity. After he retired from his trusteeship he stayed on at the office succeeding Sir Henry Dale as a senior person to watch over the potential indiscretions of the young man who had come to be in charge of the activities of the Trust. I did not find it necessary to consult him on all matters. John Boyd, because he had worked for the Foundation, had very strong insider views on the staff and style of its activities. He did not like Michael Perrin, the chairman, and sided very strongly with Bill Creasy – the President of the American Company. These personal views made Perrin's plans to make the laboratories more relevant to the Company's business very difficult. He also resisted all plans to alter the structure of the Trust that would involve raising capital through the sale of shares.

11

CHAPTER 3

The Burroughs Wellcome Company in the USA

It became apparent to the trustees in the first few years after Wellcome died that any chance of fulfilling his wishes would depend on the activities in the USA. I think, however, that it would have been beyond their wildest dreams to imagine that the American offshoot would make such important discoveries and therefore provide an income that could make the Trust so immensely rich.

A branch of Burroughs Wellcome was established in the USA and was opened in New York in 1906, just three months after the Canadian branch, and acquired offices in Hudson Street in 1907. During its first seven years it was a marketing organisation for products produced in Britain and did not make a profit until 1918. For this reason Pearson, the manager in London who was responsible for it, and his accountant S L Moore did not regard it with favour and blocked all attempts that it made to expand. Thomas Nevin from the Canadian branch was appointed President in 1911 and Henry Wellcome, possibly because of his origins, took a special interest in and often backed Nevin's plans and countermanded Pearson's decisions. During the First World War it was relatively isolated from London and Nevin grasped the opportunity to build it up. In 1925 premises for manufacture and packaging were built in Tuckahoe, New York and this together with a very active sales programme based on well trained salesmen's visits to physicians began to make the Company profitable. On Nevin's initiative a laboratory was opened and this not only monitored the quality of production but also formulated new products which further expanded sales.

During the Second World War the Company in London had been virtually taken over by the government to supply the needs of the services and replace the products for medicine that had previously been supplied from abroad. The American company was the only part of the Company that was able to make a profit until after the war and so concentration in America may have been a positive initiative from London!

In 1945 Nevin retired and was succeeded by William Creasy. Creasy was to become a dominant President for the next seventeen years. He had been with the Company since the age of 22 when he graduated from pharmacy school and had persuaded Nevin to allow him a trial as an assistant salesman on the road. He was very successful at this in New York and before long was put in charge of sales in California. After that he returned to New York as assistant sales manager and in 1934 became involved in business research and statistics and made many improvements in the Company's management. In 1943 he became general manager of the Canadian Company and two years later was made President of the US Company in succession to Nevin.

Creasy's life had been made by the Wellcome Company. He was a man of great vigour. He loved the Company and used to greet all the employees at the gate in the morning by their first names. He drove the Company's sales particularly of tabloid Empirin, which became a best seller contributing almost two-thirds of the Company's earnings for many years. He encouraged the research laboratories and especially George Hitchings who had been appointed head of biochemistry in 1942. When Henry Dale visited New York Creasy gave him a royal welcome and thereafter Henry Dale respected him. John Boyd also visited him when he was head of the Wellcome Laboratories of Tropical Medicine and they became great friends. Creasy thus had two admirers on the board of trustees and by this time he believed that he could do as he liked as the London Company had become so dependent on the US Company. When he disagreed with London he would threaten to resign. This went on for a number of years but eventually, in 1962 after Dale had retired, his threat to resign was accepted by the board in London. Creasy had made the Company in the USA but when I met him towards the end of his presidency I realised how he was probably beginning to damage the Company. He was succeeded by Fred Coe, a more balanced man who masterminded the relocation from Tuckahoe to Research Triangle Park near Raleigh, Durham in North Carolina and led the Company forward on the back of the discoveries by

George Hitchings, Trudy Elion and Howard Schaeffer.

The research laboratories concentrated at first on producing new formulations for sale to the public. An important one of these was Dexin, an artificial milk substitute for bottle feeding of babies which was highly recommended by paediatricians. The team led by Baltzy and Beer undertook pharmacodynamic research and AP Phillips synthesised suxamethonium, a short acting neuromuscular blocking agent which could be used in anaesthesia when tubocurarine (the refined South American arrow poison developed by the Wellcome laboratories in England) lasted too long.

Methoxamine (Vasoxyl), a sympathomimetic vasoconstrictor, was discovered and used for the treatment of hypotension and paroxysmal tachycardia. An original method for testing antihistaminic and bronchodilator activity led to the discovery in 1947 of Cyclizine, which as Marzine is still used as a remedy for motion sickness. Cyclizine was found to be useful in controlling the emetic action of morphine. Chlorcyclizine (Histantin) was produced as a more persistent antihistaminic and was among the more popular drugs of this type until it was superseded by Actidil as a major Burroughs Wellcome product.

George Hitchings was in charge of research in biochemistry. At first he was the only member of the department and his interest was in the nucleic acids, the building blocks for cell replication and growth. These molecules are essential for the growth of all living cells whether they be parasites, bacteria, cancers or viruses, as well as all animals including man. He realised that if he could make compounds which would interfere with nucleic acid synthesis he might use them to stop the multiplication and growth of cancer cells, bacteria and parasites. There was also another significant difference between parasites and animals. The former made folic acid, an essential vitamin, whereas animals had to obtain their supply of it from foods. He realised that if he could exploit these differences he could kill parasites that were affecting man and animals. He also initiated research to try and make molecules that would block folic acid synthesis but would not affect animals.

In 1944 he was joined by Trudy Elion, a chemistry graduate who soon learned from him all he knew about nucleic acids and his ideas. Together they set about making chemicals for testing in models of various diseases. They were aware that molecules with the structures called purines and pyrimidines have some effect on cell growth. It was now necessary to have some way of testing their new compounds. Hitchings recruited Elvira Falco from the department of bacteriology at Wellcome to set up suitable screens. She developed a culture of *lactobacillus caseii* from which they could tell if their compounds had any effect on bacterial replication. For cancer they enlisted the cooperation of the Sloan Kettering Institute which bred mice with leukaemia and other tumours. A hint from the structure of an anti-malarial, proguanil, made them think that malaria might be a possible target and this they were able to have tested by Len Goodwin in the Wellcome Laboratories of Tropical Medicine in London. Effects were shown on malaria and the compound pyrimethamine (Daraprim) was developed. Trimethoprim had antibiotic properties and when combined with a sulphonamide was marketed as Septrin primarily for urinary infections. Mercaptopurine caused remissions in childhood leukaemia. Azathioprine (imuran) depressed antibody production which led to its use in organ trans-plantation, allopurinol lowered blood uric acid and was effective for the treatment of gout. Later Howard Schaeffer, who joined the others when they moved to North Carolina, in 1971, undertook studies that pointed the way for the development of antivirals for herpes infections (acyclovir) and AIDS (zidovudine).

I met George Hitchings on several occasions and heard him talk about his work. I interviewed Trudy Elion and Howard Schaeffer in 1997. The following pages are based on George Hitchings's Nobel Prize Oration and my interviews with Elion and Schaeffer. Hitchings and Elion shared a Nobel Prize for their research in 1988.

Dr George Hitchings

George Hitchings was born in Hoquiam, Washington in 1905 where his father was a shipbuilder who died after a long illness when George was twelve. The deep impression made on him and his thoughts caused him to turn towards medicine. This objective shaped his selection of courses in high school and expressed itself in his graduation oration for which he chose the life of Louis Pasteur. The blending of Pasteur's basic research and practical results remained a goal throughout his career.

He entered the University of Washington as a premedical student in 1923 but found the enthusiasm of faculty and students in the chemistry department so infectious that by the end of the first year he had transferred to becoming a chemistry Major and obtained his degree in 1927. He stayed for a further year to obtain his Master's in 1928. For further graduate work he went to Harvard and after one year as a teaching fellow in the Department of Chemistry he was accepted as a Teaching Fellow in the Department of Biological Chemistry in the Harvard Medical School. He was assigned to Cyrus Fiske and became caught up in the Fiske-Subbarow programme. This group discovered phosphocreatinine and later adenosine triphosphate. He was assigned to prepare physiological studies using micro methods for the purine bases. These methods constituted his dissertation for his PhD in 1933. That was the time of the Great Depression and he then experienced nine years of intellectual and financial impermanence. In 1942 he joined the Wellcome Research Laboratories in Tuckahoe, New York and soon after Elvira Falco joined him. Trudy Elion followed in 1944 and Peter Russell in 1947. Elion took part in most of the projects dealing with purines, and Falco participated in everything from bacteriology and animal feeding to organic chemistry. Under the leadership of Falco, a constant flow of banter developed covering a wide range of subjects and degrees of seriousness.

In 1947 they began to send compounds to the Sloan Kettering Institute to be screened for activity against acute leukaemia. Among the first compounds tested was 2,6-diaminopurine, which proved active and later produced several notable remissions.

The association with the Sloan Kettering was a major influence for growth. They were offered financial support to enable them to increase their search for anti-tumor agents. C P Rhoads the director had realised that their compounds were of special interest intrinsically and they were supported by a package of biological information. The external help allowed the laboratory to expand to a team of 15. In 1948 responsibility for the purine and pyrimidine compounds was divided between Trudy Elion and Hitchings and Falco and Russell took charge of the studies of an antifolic acid compound p-chlorophenoxy-2,4diaminopyrimidine.

From 1967 George Hitchings was made Vice-President in charge of research at Burroughs Wellcome and by 1968 was very involved with the move to North Carolina.

George Hitchings contribution to Burroughs Wellcome and indirectly to the Wellcome Trust and medical research was immense.

Dr Trudy Elion

Trudy Elion was born and bred in New York and went to graduate college there to study chemistry. Her father was a dentist and they lived in the vicinity of Tuckahoe where the Burroughs, Wellcome Company was located. She had vowed since she was fifteen to be a scientist and to find a cure for cancer. At that time it was not easy to get a job in science other than school teaching and she did that for a while. She was, however, determined to get a job in a laboratory and one day her father suggested that she might try BW which was nearby and might have a laboratory. He knew nothing about them except that they gave him tablets of Empirin to give to patients he had treated. She had never heard of them but she telephoned and asked if they had a laboratory and by any chance might they have a job. Well, they said, as a matter of fact we have. They said that she could come to be interviewed on Saturday morning. She duly arrived and George Hitchings interviewed her and gave her a job. This was 1944 and George had been there a couple of years.

She said there was an atmosphere about the place that was almost like academia. If you were keen you could develop your own ideas. George was studying nucleic acids and she had been employed to work with him. She learned very rapidly and he gave her the opportunity to develop her own ideas.

The laboratory was quite small and the biochemical department which George headed was essentially three people, himself and two assistants. They were at a very exciting era of biochemistry when DNA was still not firmly established as genetic material but they did know that cells had to have it to divide. Their outlook was to find a way to stop DNA synthesis and then look for the kinds of cells that they wanted to destroy

When the laboratory moved to Research Triangle Park, North Carolina there was more space and they could work more rapidly and study the biochemistry and pharmacology of their compounds. They were provided with whatever they needed. (The funding of research in North Carolina was provided from the earnings of the Company in the USA and was not subject to decisions in London). In 1968 the researchers turned to the viruses. The stimulus was a paper about adenine arabinoside which is a purine nucleoside. They made diaminopurine arabinoside and that was the beginning of the antivirals. They sent this compound to John Bauer in London who was working on the Thiosemicarbazones. They were getting on quite well with the arabinosides and preparing for clinical trials when Howard Schaeffer arrived at RTP with a different type of nucleoside. When John Bauer tested his compounds they showed great activity.

Trudy Elion was a delightful person and a joy to know. As has been noted elsewhere she was awarded a Nobel Prize jointly with George Hitchings.

Dr Howard Schaeffer

Howard Schaeffer was born and brought up in Rochester, New York where about 70% of the population worked for Kodak. While he was undertaking his undergraduate work in pharmacy at the University of Buffalo he knew that he wanted to go beyond a bachelor's degree. He debated whether he should go into medicine or dentistry but it wasn't until he was a senior that he found that chemistry was his real love. He said " There is an art to it that is very difficult to explain to people who are not chemists. It is the joy that comes from a completed project with clean answers to problems that you set out to solve."

At first, for his Master's degree at the University of Florida he worked in plant chemistry on the active ingredient in the Manchineel tree that grows in the Everglades. It produces blisters in unwary beachgoers. For his PhD degree he had a fellowship from the Institute of Nuclear Studies in Oakridge, Tennessee. This was in the early days of the field when you couldn't buy radio-labelled chemicals. He was one of the few people who actually synthesized benzene from carbon dioxide. The two starting materials were Carbon 14 labelled carbon dioxide and Carbon 14 labelled cyanide. He made about a gram of C14 benzene which enabled him to make organic mechanism studies.

Howard Schaeffer was always interested in looking for anti-cancer and anti-viral agents and the two types of molecule which are very active are in the category of heterocycles and nucleosides. His interest in cancer was stimulated by his first job at The Southern Research Institute in Birmingham, Alabama. He was working in Alabama with people who had contracts from the National Cancer Institute.

His next appointment was as a member of the faculty at the University of Buffalo to organise a department of medicinal chemistry. He built the department up to ten people. At first he was rather busy but after a couple of years he had an NIH Career Development Award which meant that he had a fair amount of time for research as he only had to give 20 to 30 lectures a year. He stayed there from 1959 to 1970 when he left to join Burroughs Wellcome. This was a very productive time during which he became more and more involved in heterocyclic molecules.

Howard Schaeffer met George Hitchings at an international symposium at the University of Nijmegen in The Netherlands. When they went back to America George invited him to come down to Burroughs Wellcome to give a lecture. From that visit it became clear that the Company was going to move and he was offered the position as Head of Chemical Research. The Company did not move for a couple of years and during this time he used to consult for them at Tuckahoe.

When he joined BW in North Carolina he wrote a research proposal of what he wanted to do and what he was interested in. In that proposal he indicated that he was trying to make compounds that would have either anti-viral or anti-cancer activity. He had not tested any of his compounds as he did not have the facilities to do this in Buffalo. In this proposal he indicated the types of compounds that he would like to make. He showed George Hitchings the proposal and he made a very interesting comment. He said that it wouldn't really do any good to inhibit a virus because by the time the symptoms appear in a human most the viral damage has already been done but continued that if he really wanted to work on these, then go ahead. So he went back to his lab and started a series of studies of what are now called acyclic nucleotides. From that study eventually he obtained Zovirax (acyclovir).

At that time they did not think of them as anti-virals and did not have any clear indication of their activity until he sent John Bauer in England a compound that he had made at Buffalo which was called 71-3 and that came back showing some activity and so they continued to manipulate the molecule and explore various chemical changes until they came up with 134 and then eventually 248 which is Zovirax, which was 100 times more effective. They did the toxicology very rapidly and then set up a project and moved it forward as fast as they could.

Trudy Elion along with Paul Demeranda and Phil Furman then worked out how Zovirax acted to kill the herpes virus. They found that when herpes invades a cell, during the first 6-8 hours it develops two new enzymes that are herpes-coded and these are thymidine kinase and DNA polymerase. It so happens that Zovirax is activated by the herpes thymidine kinase and then becomes a DNA polymerase inhibitor. But in the normal cells that also have human thymidine kinase the acyclic Zovirax is not activated by the human thymidine kinase so it has very great selectivity. The reason why the toxicity of the compound was so low was because it is only activated in those cells that are infected with herpes.

Initially it was difficult to get Zovirax approved for use in patients. This was because all of the earlier anti-viral agents had sprung from anti-cancer programmes. So it took some negotiations and arguments for several months before the Food and Drug Administration finally agreed to permit clinical trials. Once the trials got going and there was no toxicity things began to move very rapidly and Zovirax became the fourth best selling drug in the world.

The Trust made a grant of US$2million in the name of Howard Schaeffer to the University of Arizona in Tuscon in recognition of his contribution to the discovery of antiviral drugs, the sale of which led to the great wealth of the Wellcome Trust. In the citation he was commended not only as a scientist but as a delightful, amusing and caring person.

The Burroughs Wellcome Fund

Bill Creasy, President of Burroughs Wellcome USA, drew Henry Dale's attention to an American statute that permitted a commercial company to be relieved of tax for charitable donations. Dale agreed that the American company should take up this option and so in 1955 the Burroughs Wellcome Fund was established. This allowed the trustees to ensure that the success of the American Company resulted in some funds being made available locally without applications having to be sent to London.

After the enormously successful share sale of 1992 a small dinner was held at Wilton's Restaurant in London. At the dinner the then Chairman of the Trust told Howard Schaeffer that the Trust would like to give a capital sum of US$400 million to the Burroughs Wellcome Fund in recognition of Sir Henry Wellcome's origin and the great contribution that Burroughs Wellcome had made to the Trust over many years. In a charming reply Howard said, "It did cross our minds that we in the States had played our part in the Wellcome success story. To be told tonight that you are giving US$400 million which would take the BW Fund into the top 50 of US charities is beyond our wildest dreams. It is so inspired of you at the Trust to be so generous. You could have got away with $100 million ... no you couldn't."

In 1997 a meeting under my chairmanship was held in Raleigh Durham at which the donation was formally recognized. Present at the meeting were Sir David Steel, Sir Roger Gibbs, Sir Stanley Peart and Dr Julian Jack from the Trust and Trudy Elion, Howard Schaeffer and Martha Peck from the Fund. The video and transcript is a historical vignette of key people in the Wellcome story.

CHAPTER 4

The Wellcome Company
in the United Kingdom

In Chapter 2, I left the story of the Company in England in 1945 to cross the Atlantic and describe how the US subsidiary Burroughs Wellcome and Company had managed its affairs so well as to become highly profitable and a household name in the pharmaceutical world. Now I must return to London and take up the story of the period from 1945 to 1980. As was only too evident in 1945 the Company was at such a low ebb that its borrowings from the bank amounted to more than a year's turnover. The task was to re-establish the Company so that it could become profitable. To do this the research laboratories had to discover new medicines and the Company had to improve its capacity to manufacture and sell these discoveries as well as those from America.

The changing of the laboratories from programmes focussed on the interests of individuals into a programme aimed at new products was not easy because Dale and Boyd, with their veto as trustees, wished to preserve the academic approach that had been established by Henry Wellcome. On the commercial side capital was needed for reconstruction and development of factories and sales arrangements at home and overseas. A suggestion to sell shares in Wellcome was examined during Lord Piercy's chairmanship but this was not pursued.

The research laboratories were gradually moved towards a more commercial approach and the discoveries of DW Adamson led to a number of profitable products. None of these discoveries in Britain yielded enough profit to allow the scale of growth that took place. In addition the Company was still the owner of Wellcome's Historical Collections which were a considerable financial burden. In 1960 these were sold to the Trust using a special tax-free dividend of £3,030,000 but the Company still continued to pay for their annual upkeep and costs.

The finances of the Wellcome Company 1967–85

During the years 1965-85 there were three chairmen of the Company: Sir Michael Perrin to 1970, Andy Gray to 1977 and Alfred Shepperd to 1985, three years after Franks retired and the year of the first sale of shares. During this time the profits after tax rose from £5m to £121m but the distribution to the Trust grew very slowly until the 1980s.

The following schedule is a summary of financial information over a period of nineteen years to 1985, the year immediately before the flotation which took place on 14 February 1986. This information has been extracted from the Annual Report and Accounts of the Wellcome Foundation Limited prepared on a consolidated basis, as filed in Companies House.

The figures and financial commentary that follow have been prepared by Philip Bradley who played such a key part in the long relationship between Flemings and the Trust. They show the whole picture.

Philip Bradley makes the following observations:

1 The Company delivered a strong and consistent rate of growth both in sales and profits over the period and as one would expect from this sector of industry there were no detectable influences from economic circumstances.

2 Research and Development expenditure increased over the period both as a percentage of turnover and pre R & D profits, reaching a relatively steady state over the last five years of 12% and 50% respectively. This was in line with other major pharmaceutical companies at that time.

3 From the funds generated by the business a significant and increasing amount was used for capital expenditure on manufacturing plant and buildings and R & D facilities as might reasonably be expected from a company in this industry with its growth in size and profitability.

4 In addition to capital expenditure a significant amount of the cash generated was employed in the growth of working capital complementing the growth in the overall business and in paying varying rates of corporation tax.

Wellcome Foundation Ltd Financial Summary

	1967	1968	1969	1970	1971	1972	1973	1974	1975	1976	1977	1978	1979	1980	1981	1982	1983	1984	1985
Profit and Loss (£m)																			
Sales to Outside Customers	50.5	62.5	75.1	85.7	96.6	113.0	140.2	173.5	212.9	290.2	341.8	381.7	411.6	442.4	500.3	592.5	674.4	806.4	1,003.6
Profit Before Tax and Development	9.2	11.3	14.0	14.4	16.4	21.5	29.6	34.3	44.9	67.4	75.4	84.5	90.7	96.6	102.1	121.4	142.1	186.1	243.7
Research and Development	2.9	3.6	4.5	5.8	7.5	8.7	9.9	11.5	15.9	23.1	29.0	33.4	39.1	47.3	52.0	66.3	80.9	96.6	122.0
Profit Before Tax	6.3	7.7	9.5	8.6	8.9	12.8	19.7	22.8	29.0	44.3	46.4	51.1	51.6	49.3	50.1	55.1	61.2	89.5	121.7
Tax and Other	2.8	4.1	4.9	4.0	4.3	5.3	9.8	11.6	15.2	21.6	24.5	27.6	27.8	12.2	17.0	18.0	23.3	43.6	53.0
Profit After Tax	3.3	4.5	2.6	4.2	3.6	6.0	9.4	12.7	14.3	19.9	21.9	24.5	23.4	37.1	33.1	36.3	37.9	46.2	68.7
Distribution to the Trust	1.5	1.6	1.9	2.1	2.1	2.5	2.5	2.8	3.0	3.7	5.6	7.0	9.0	9.0	10.5	13.0	14.0	17.0	23.8
Retained Profit	1.8	2.9	0.7	2.1	1.5	3.5	6.9	9.9	11.3	16.5	16.3	16.4	16.2	27.4	22.6	23.6	23.6	28.6	44.9
Cash Flow (£m)																			
Funds Generated	N/A	N/A	N/A	N/A	N/A	N/A	N/A	N/A	N/A	28.7	35.5	39.1	40.8	52.2	60.8	61.4	89.1	128.0	184.3
CAPEX	N/A	N/A	N/A	N/A	N/A	N/A	N/A	N/A	N/A	17.6	20.0	20.8	27.0	26.0	40.9	41.4	38.5	55.7	80.0
Distribution to Trust	N/A	N/A	N/A	N/A	N/A	N/A	N/A	N/A	N/A	3.7	5.6	6.6	7.4	10.0	10.5	13.0	14.0	17.0	23.8
"Tax, Working Capital and Other"	N/A	N/A	N/A	N/A	N/A	N/A	N/A	N/A	N/A	7.6	18.0	8.9	11.1	28.8	16.4	2.9	37.0	65.2	92.9
Increase/decrease in borrowing	N/A	N/A	N/A	N/A	N/A	N/A	N/A	N/A	N/A	-0.2	-8.1	-2.8	-4.7	-12.6	-7.0	4.1	-0.4	-11.9	22.6
Net Indebtedness																			
Loan Capital	N/A	N/A	N/A	N/A	N/A	N/A	N/A	N/A	N/A	42.5	55.3	42.9	71.1	79.3	86.3	82.1	82.5	94.4	78.1
Capital Employed	N/A	N/A	N/A	N/A	N/A	N/A	N/A	N/A	N/A	180.8	215.4	218.6	232.3	255.3	302.1	326.8	368.1	420.6	438.6
Statistics																			
Research and Development																			
as % of Turnover	4.0%	5.0%	5.7%	6.2%	7.8%	7.2%	6.4%	6.5%	7.1%	7.9%	8.5%	8.7%	9.5%	10.7%	10.4%	11.2%	11.9%	12.0%	12.1%
as % of pre R&D Turnover	22.2%	22.8%	22.6%	0.4%	43.7%	38.0%	31.0%	32.3%	34.1%	34.3%	38.5%	39.5%	43.1%	49.0%	50.9%	54.6%	56.9%	51.9%	50.1%
Distributions to Trust																			
as % of post-tax profits	44.9%	35.6%	71.4%	50.0%	57.8%	41.5%	26.3%	26.7%	21.7%	21.2%	18.6%	25.6%	29.9%	24.2%	31.7%	35.8%	36.9%	36.7%	34.6%
as % of cash funds generated	N/A	N/A	N/A	N/A	N/A	N/A	N/A	N/A	N/A	12.9%	15.8%	16.9%	18.1%	19.2%	17.3%	21.2%	15.7%	13.3%	12.9%

Notes:

The above has been extracted from the auditors consolidated accounts of the Wellcome Foundation for the relevant years. Arithmetical differences may occur due to minor adjustments, which are not material to the overall financial record.

Distributions are gross up to 1972 and from 1973 onwards are net of imputed tax credit.

In 1980, when the Company was thriving, it celebrated its Centenary. A publication *In Pursuit of Excellence* was produced that told the story in more detail. The following section and the story in Chapter 11 is based on this publication.

The Expansion of the Wellcome Company 1950–80

During the thirty years from 1950 the Wellcome Company grew at a quite spectacular rate. It started the three decade period with a limited international presence and product range. In 1950 the sales of the Company were less than £10 million. By 1980 this picture had changed dramatically. The Company's sales turnover had grown to more than £400 million per annum and it had developed a significant operating presence in almost all major world markets. In 1980 the Americas represented 38% of the company's turnover, 29% in the combined regions of Africa, Asia and Australia with 18% in Europe and 15% in the UK.

The success of the company during this period was fuelled not only by its expanded market presence, but by a steady stream of important new products. These new products were the result of considerable investments that had been made in targeted, strategically important research programmes. During this time the company did not restrict itself to a narrow range of health improvement areas. Wellcome products encompassed innovative medicines and vaccines for human as well as veterinary health care together with a variety of diagnostic agents, insecticides and industrial hygiene products.

The company's success was a result of the board's insighted long-term strategy and the dedication of senior managers and scientific experts throughout the company. The marked expansion in the range and sales volume of its products brought a new set of issues that had to be managed. There was a need for large-scale capital investment in plant and infrastructure. This investment was able to be financed from organic growth and the significant revenues contributed by "Empirin" in the USA. By 1980 more than twenty manufacturing sites around the world were producing products to satisfy the new levels of demand.

The board had three key strategic objectives during this period. The first was to increase corporate turnover and net revenue. It did this by strengthening the commercial awareness of the Company and its marketing and sales expertise. In addition, during the early days of Sir Michael Perrin's chairmanship of the Company, it was agreed with the Wellcome trustees that there was an overriding commercial need to re-invest the profits of the Company back into the organisation in order to fund growth. To this end, during the 30 years from 1950 to 1980 almost 70% of the net profits of the Company were re-invested and not distributed to shareholders, namely the Wellcome Trust.

The board's second strategic objective was to expand the product range by in-house research and development as well as appropriate corporate and product acquisitions. As a result of this approach the pipeline produced a steady stream of commercially important medicines and vaccines. The level of research innovation and marketing success was particularly fruitful during the late 1960s with the introductions of "Septrin" and "Zyloric".

Improved life-cycle management of the established products in the portfolio became increasingly important in order to finance the support for the new products as they found their place in the expanding world markets. Cyclizine, which was first marketed as "Marzine", a travel sickness remedy, was combined with ergotamine tartrate to create "Migril". Migril became commercially important as a treatment for migraine. "Actidil", a potent antihistamine used for the treatment of hay fever, was re-formulated with other compounds to create the very successful "Actifed" range of cough and cold remedies.

The board's third objective was to increase the Company's international market presence and penetration. Achieving this was critical, not only to increase much needed revenues, but to balance the exposure risks of the Company away from its reliance on the UK market. At the turn of the 1950s there were only eight associated Wellcome companies, with product manufacture taking place in only four of them. By 1979 the picture had changed considerably with sixty significant subsidiary companies and five associated companies. The first purchase in 1959 was of Cooper, McDougall & Robertson Limited. This acquisition not only brought vital expansion of international trading relationships but strengthened the existing veterinary range of Wellcome products.

Prior to 1960 Wellcome had a very limited presence in Europe. Of course the company was very strong in the UK, but the company had a presence in only one other European country – Italy. During the 1960s operations were established in seven other European countries and a further four were added between 1970 and 1979. This European expansion was mirrored with the formation of many operating companies in East Africa and South

East Asia. The initial tactic was to establish relationships with local agents and once critical mass had been reached incorporate the operations into a local Wellcome company. This business approach was driven by Dr Fred Wrigley who joined the Wellcome board in 1957 as sales director and retired as deputy chairman of the Company in 1974.

There were concerns at the time that the international expansion and establishment of overseas production facilities would harm UK exports. However these concerns proved unfounded as the opening of vigorous new markets and expansion of the product range resulted in an increase in the volume and value of UK exports.

To support the Company during this period of dynamic growth it was clear that changes had to be made to the structures of the organisation which, at that time, operated largely independently of each other. Under the chairmanship of Sir Michael Perrin (1953-1970) the Company was restructured into a single, co-ordinated organisation. In 1967 three deputy chairmen were appointed. Dr DE Wheeler, who was formerly the managing-director, had the role to co-ordinate all central group activities such as research and development, production and finance. Dr Fred Wrigley became the head of medical sales with responsibility for the overseas companies and was also the chairman of the Calmic Company. Mr AA Gray took on the responsibility for all world-wide veterinary sales and was the chairman of Cooper, McDougall & Robertson. In addition to these changes a regional management structure was put in place. Regional managers were appointed for the world's major geographical markets and a central marketing function was established. This critical transformation continued to evolve further under the subsequent leadership of Mr Andy Gray who was chairman from 1971 to 1977 and Mr Alfred Shepperd who succeeded Mr Gray on the latter's retirement in 1977.

During these 30 years considerable investment was made in the UK to modernise and extend the research laboratories based in Beckenham, Kent. This work was essential, not only because of the growing sophistication of the research being undertaken, but also because of the need to satisfy the increasingly onerous regulatory requirements. The company's main production facility at Dartford in Kent was in great need of modernisation and expansion of its manufacturing capacity. Almost half of the buildings on the site in 1950 were either demolished or downgraded and used for other purposes. At the end of this re-development the facilities on the site had trebled. The production site at Crewe in Cheshire was also modernised and became the company's second largest production site. New manufacturing facilities were built in Brazil, Mexico, Nigeria, Pakistan and New Zealand. Other sites in Australia, Belgium, India, Italy, Spain, South Africa and West Germany were completely re-built, extended or re-located. All of these changes were essential for the company to manage the substantial growth it was undergoing. Probably the most significant infrastructure change during this period was the move of the US company from Tuckahoe, New York to two sites in North Carolina.

The evident success of the board's strategy for carefully planned growth is clear, but it should not be forgotten that it depended on the availability of one exceedingly important factor: money! This growth required a very great deal of money. As a private company finance could not be raised from the stock market. The agreement at the time between the board and the trustees of the Wellcome Trust that the profits of the company should be re-invested cannot be understated. It was vital that the profits resulting from the tremendous commercial success of new products such as "Septrin" and "Zyloric" be used to sustain the company's very ambitious expansion plans.

Sir Alfred Shepperd

Alfred Shepperd (always spoken of as Shep but only used as a form of address by a few) was appointed finance director of the Wellcome Foundation Limited in 1972 and became its chairman and chief executive in 1977. After the flotation of the Company in 1986 he was the chairman and chief executive of Wellcome plc until he retired in 1990.

Shep was born in 1925 and read economics at University College, London. His business career between 1949 and 1972 was spent in the Rank Organisation (entertainment), Selincourt (textiles), Keyser Ullman (merchant bank) and Laporte (chemicals). He was described in his obituary as a formidable businessman, combative and a workaholic.

As chairman of the Wellcome Foundation Limited he presided over the phase when the Company was reaping the benefits of the great discoveries of profitable medicinal products. He therefore had ample funds to invest in its research and development and the restructuring of the Company and the spreading of its manufacturing and sales capacity all over the world.

He was nominated to be chairman by the board of the Company which had only one non-executive director, Lord Greenhill, a retired diplomat who had been a colleague of Oliver Franks when he was Ambassador in Washington. The appointment of the chairman was in the hands of the trustees and Shep was the only possible internal candidate. The trustees knew very little about him.

Franks, after consulting Greenhill, supported the proposal and the trustees accepted his opinion. No one suggested a wider search for anyone else with experience of research in industry.

Shepperd did not appoint a finance director when he became chairman but continued in that role. He dominated the board and was not averse to threatening tactics as I experienced once when, having unburdened himself to me about the director of research, he said he would get me sacked if I mentioned our conversation to anyone. This characteristic was known especially to Stan Peart and me because after dinner at the first policy meeting of the Trust that Shepperd attended he stayed up late with the two of us and described the domineering management style which he proposed to use now he was chairman. Unfortunately he did not have any insight into the way in which scientists thought and worked, such an important element for the chairman of the board of a pharmaceutical company and especially needed for Wellcome in England which had a tradition of academic research initiated by Wellcome and directed by Sir John Vane an academic pharmacologist. Vane was the only scientist on the board of the Company. Shepperd could only see research as the discovery of products for sale.

Vane, who I knew very well before he joined the Company, used to meet me frequently to discuss his problems but I could do little more than say that whatever he felt about Sir Henry Wellcome's intentions for the Beckenham laboratories they were there to produce products for the Company to sell. He could not appeal to the Trustees about Henry Wellcome's intentions because the laboratories were not the responsibility of the Trust after Wellcome died and the Trustees would not arbitrate between him and the chairman of the Company. Of course it was unavoidable to make comparisons with the commercial successes being reaped from the discoveries in America. These problems all came to a head in the middle 1980's with the result that

Vane and Black, both Nobel Prize winners left the Company.

Franks described Shepperd as having a good financial brain and being a good salesman (presumably because he could sell his plans to Franks). Shepperd described his relations with Franks to me when I interviewed him in 1996 as follows:

"I found him really easy to deal with. I think that is almost a tribute to the way he made it easy. I can remember very early on I said to Oliver; 'we can't always guarantee that our interests will coincide' and he was well over six foot and he looked down at me and said 'My dear Shep it will be alright if we are honest with one another. We became good friends and after he retired the contact was maintained."

When David Steel took over he described an early meeting with Shepperd: I think Shepperd saw the Trust as a body that distributed the largesse given to it by the Company from its earnings rather than as owners of the Company that existed to supply funds for the philanthropic activities stipulated in Henry Wellcome's will.

The relationship between Shepperd and Steel and Gibbs became strained during the sale process.

I have written this account for the record but the figures show that during Shepperd's chairmanship the Company prospered greatly. Shepperd was knighted in 1989.

CHAPTER 5

Lord Franks as Chairman
of the Trust

1965 was the watershed year for the Wellcome Trust. It coincided with the appointment of Lord Franks of Headington as the chairman, a position he was to occupy for the next 17 years. Although I intend to describe this period around Franks's role I must emphasise that the changes only came to pass because the successes in the research of the Company created the funds with which the business could expand and provide a sizeable regular dividend which could be used to plan and develop the charitable activities of the Trust.

Franks separated the activities of the Trust into two parts: the relations with the pharmaceutical Company which he took on himself as a dialogue with the Company chairman and the support of research. It must have been a delight for successive Company chairmen to have such a large amount of money available for development. Franks did not press for a higher dividend for the Trust because, in his view, it was not ripe to handle such larger sums of money which was in the meanwhile likely to provide better returns if left in the business. The Company chairmen were protected from the demand from shareholders, the Wellcome trustees, complaining about the dividend largely because Franks's headmaster-like presence brooked any argument on the subject. There was one other trustee who might have lessened the dominance of Franks, Bobby Nesbitt, a solicitor who had succeeded the obligatory solicitor, Bullock, named in the will. He did not however raise his voice. When he retired he was succeeded by Lord Murray, a university administrator who was also not knowledgeable about commercial finance. When Price, the accountant trustee, retired he was replaced by a scientist as one was needed and Franks did not think anyone else was required for his dealings with the Company.

Sir Stanley Peart summed up the trustees' position in the following words: "The trustees were led by the feeling that Franks knew best and most of us were not familiar with the real workings of the Company. The Annual General Meeting was of little value and we were happy for a long time to accept Franks' assessment of what we could expect. We were not knowledgeable, or querulous, enough to challenge the chairman to justify the arrangements – sadly most of us had other activities which occupied our minds and critical faculties!"

I think it reasonable to criticize Franks for not having seen that more funds were made available to the Trust earlier. It certainly could have been afforded by the Company – especially during the last 5 years of his chairmanship between 1977 and 1982. The dividend remained at around 30% of the profits after tax. I was left with the impression that he did not think the academic scientific world would produce returns as important as the company with the successes in the USA as his benchmark. Measured by financial return this was of course true because universities did not plan to make marketable discoveries

Of course Franks would not have wanted to launch such a major operation as selling shares in opposition to the wishes of Shepperd in his final years – especially when his chairmanship was extended by two years because of the untimely death of Lord Armstrong of Sanderstead, who was to be his successor.

For, the second function, the philanthropic activities and administration Franks appointed me as Secretary and later Director responsible to the board of trustees. The Scientific Trustees and I set about making plans for the support of medical research using a budget of £1m a year which at that time was quite a healthy sum. As the Trust settled into its policy it was able to see how larger sums could be spent.

Lord Franks

The general description of Lord Franks in Oxford was that "behind that chest of steel beats a heart of ice". He certainly was a very forbidding figure and although we became reasonably relaxed in one another's company I always sensed this dominance. This may have been partly because he was by nature a university tutor and always looked at everything one wrote as if it was an undergraduate essay, to be improved, a forbidding approach.

However, he came to the Trust like a breath of fresh air. He recognised that the state of affairs created by the senility of the trustees was a disgrace and he set about reforming the arrangements very quickly. On the trustees' side, he had Sir John McMichael, who was an ideal scientific member. Otherwise, the elderly group that had been there when I arrived had all by now retired. He was, therefore, able to recruit a new and younger group, including Professor Robert Thompson and Professor Henry Barcroft.

His other main change was to recognize that the secretaryship of the Trust could now transfer to its office in Queen Anne Street and be undertaken by me, in addition to my duties as Scientific Secretary. Jack Clarke continued to look after the financial affairs of the Trust from Viney, Price & Goodyear, the accountants.

During Franks's time, the trustees held one of their first policy meetings. I recount the manner of this to give an illustration of Franks's style. I had prepared a paper on policy worked out over many months and after detailed discussion with the scientists on the board of trustees, Franks had accepted it and it had been circulated to the trustees. At the meeting held at Frant, near Tunbridge Wells, Franks went round all the trustees, and my recently appointed deputy Edda Hanington, and asked them each to express their views on policy. He made no reference to the paper. Each of them did so in their own idiosyncratic way. He did not ask me to express my views. He then closed the meeting and asked me how I thought it had gone. I expressed some disquiet, thinking that my paper had been ignored. He said "Wait till tomorrow".

Next morning when the meeting started, with no notes in front of him, he said to the trustees "I think that yesterday we agreed that the following lines of policy should be developed" and he recited some ten or so items. Everybody nodded their head, feeling very proud that they had contributed these ideas for the development of the Trust's policy and greatly admiring Franks' ability to bring their disparate remarks to such a logical conclusion. They were of course the ideas in the paper approved by the scientists and sent to all the Trustees but no reference was ever made to their origin. His impressive ability to sum up a discussion so that the conclusion was totally acceptable to all those present was a matter of great envy to anyone who did not have these skills. Franks was a much respected leader of the Trust during the seventeen years of his chairmanship.

I naturally got to know Franks very well in my many meetings with him and, after he retired, I used to visit him at home. While he always made me feel a bit intimidated I nevertheless, knew that he really was a kindly and generous man of overwhelming integrity. Lady Franks was a charming down-to-earth woman and he could not have had a wife like that unless he had human qualities! I remember visiting him at the time of his Falkland Inquiry and also when he had recently had cataract operations on his eyes. On these occasions he was probably more human than when dealing with him on business matters.

Lord Armstrong

Lord Armstrong of Sanderstead was recruited at the suggestion of Lord Franks to succeed him as Chairman of the Trust. He had, of course, been head of the Civil Service and a very dominant personality behind the Edward Heath Government. When he retired from the Civil Service he became the Chairman of the Midland Bank and therefore added to the Trust a financial background that would be useful to it in its relationship with the Company. He, therefore, as a trustee, was particularly concerned with discussions with the Foundation about their activities and the appropriate dividend for the Trust. He felt very strongly that the Company was getting away very cheaply and at one meeting at which Franks was present, he wrung out of Shepperd the promise that he would increase the dividend during the next three years by £1, £2, and £3 million per annum respectively. Franks when he spoke to me the next day was obviously annoyed, but they paid up. This growth meant that the Trust was able to expand its activities as a consequence of his pressure. Unfortunately, he died suddenly from a ruptured aortic aneurysm at a dinner at Ditchley Park and so, the succession to the chairmanship had to be rethought.

CHAPTER 6

The Support of Medical Research

As I have mentioned, when Lord Franks became Chairman of the Trust in 1965 I was appointed Secretary and, two years later, Director of the Trust. I had joined the Trust's staff in 1960 and risen to be Scientific Secretary when my predecessor Frank Green retired early on account of his health. This position as the head of administration gave me the responsibility to propose a policy for the allocation of the funds for the support of medical research and medical history. By this time I had spent 10 years in the administration of medical research on the staff of the Medical Research Council (MRC) and the Trust. Before I joined the MRC I had trained as a physician and during the previous two years had been a medical specialist at military hospitals in Germany. I had done a small amount of clinical research, written a few papers and compiled a book on Careers in Medicine. Because I had been born and largely educated in the tropics, Sir Harold Himsworth had asked me to understudy him in charge of the tropical programme of the MRC and so I had travelled to East and West Africa and the West Indies and become familiar with the research being undertaken under the aegis of the Council and the Colonial Office. This experience was just what the Trust needed on its administrative staff. Also my time at the MRC administering its university grants programme had made me familiar with a broad range of subjects and people engaged in research at all levels. One of the important parts of running a grants programme is to select suitable referees to help the Board consider applications. This knowledge can only be acquired over a wide range of subjects first from someone who has done it before and then getting to know a lot of people who are undertaking research and what they are working on. I was interested to meet these people, visit them in their places of work and hear from them about their research and so acquired a wide range of knowledge and made many friendships. I attended clinical rounds at St Mary's, Hammersmith and the Middlesex Hospital to keep me in touch with medical practice.

I was not an expert at any subject but I had a much broader experience than many. Since the scientific trustees were experts in, for instance, clinical medicine, Professor Sir John McMichael, Director of the Postgraduate Medical School; biochemistry, Professor Robert Thompson who was at Guys Hospital Medical School and Professor Henry Barcroft who held the chair of Physiology at St Thomas Hospital Medical School. I thus had very knowledgeable colleagues with whom to work out a policy for the Trust. We not only had knowledge of the subject fields but also knew the university scene in which the research was undertaken.

What I had come to realise over the past ten years was that there were large gaps in the provision for the support of research. It was not adequate to wait to see who came knocking at your door. The Trust had already, before I joined its staff, recognised that there was a dearth of research laboratories in the universities which hampered the development of ideas and the encouragement of new recruits. Furthermore major equipment such as electron microscopes and ultracentrifuges were needed and there was no source of funds to pay for them. Frank Green had suggested travel grants. So the Trust provided for these needs. From the 1960s funds for these purposes had become available from government sources in the 1960s and so the Trust could turn to other types of support.

When we cut back on major capital grants quite a lot of money was released which could be used for the support of individuals and their projects. The new policy was geared towards that type of support and we entered a more interesting activity which brought us into closer contact with research in progress. This was what stimulated our thinking. This background led to the following statement of policy which was put before the full board of trustees and published in 1966.

The Policy of the Wellcome Trust – published 1966

The income of the Wellcome Trust has increased in recent years. The trustees in consequence are now able annually to make allocations and grants on a scale which has significance, particularly in the United

Kingdom, for the shape and development of medical research. They have therefore re-examined their policy to ensure that they are using the funds at their disposal to the best advantage.

The trustees consider that one of the principal aims in the administration of the funds of the Wellcome Trust as a charitable foundation is to give flexibility to the methods by which medical research is financed.

Their intention is to support promising new advances and inadequately supported or interdisciplinary subjects which offer opportunities for development, until such time as these can be absorbed into regular budgets. They do not consider it to be their function to make up the deficiencies created in regular budgets by inadequate allocations from public funds.

The view of the Trustees on the most effective ways in which they can use the funds at their disposal is set out in the following paragraphs:

Until now the Trust has used most of its funds by way of grants to support projects put forward by individual research workers. Each application has been assessed on its scientific quality and importance, and awards have been made for those projects which were judged most promising by these criteria. The trustees intend to continue to allocate a large proportion of the funds of the Trust in this way because they believe that the mainspring of new developments will usually be the ideas of individual researchers. The basic and clinical sciences of medicine will continue to receive help as and when researchers and projects of high scientific quality can be identified.

In addition the trustees plan in future to look for investigators of high promise so that more emphasis can be given to certain selected problems. The following spheres of research give an indication of possible directions in which the Trustees could provide support.

Inadequately Supported Subjects

The progress of medical research in different fields is uneven. Some subjects which might on scientific grounds have been expected to advance rapidly have not done so. Furthermore, the emphasis of research does not always reflect the importance of a subject for human welfare, the chief objective of the Trust set out in the Founder's will. The trustees therefore will encourage research in fields giving such opportunities for development and, with the aid of qualified advisers, seek ways in which they can increase interest and performance in these fields.

Interdisciplinary Subjects

The opportunity for new advances of knowledge that can arise from linking two or more disciplines is well known: molecular biology is a current example. Such creative links are often difficult to bring about because increased specialisation reduces the number of researchers with a sufficient knowledge of more than one field. For example, the increasing emphasis of biochemists on pure organic chemistry can weaken its links with clinical medicine. In another field, increased association between ophthalmology and medicine can be of help in tackling many of the unsolved problems of the influence of general diseases on the eye. Recognising the value of such special interdisciplinary team research, the trustees will consider opportunities for its promotion, including arrangements for longer-term support where desirable.

Established Centres and Field Research Overseas

Association between established centres and work in developing countries can increase knowledge. The Trust has already organized two schemes whereby workers in this country have collaborated with colleagues abroad to study problems of mutual interest, the basic laboratory research being done in the United Kingdom and the field research abroad. Such links are leading to advances in knowledge unlikely otherwise to occur.

Endemic Tropical Diseases

The trustees have for long had a special interest in the diseases of tropical countries and have supported a number of projects overseas. They still consider that the important problems of health and disease in the tropics are insufficiently studied, largely because they occur in countries which have little money to devote to research. The trustees hope therefore to devise means by which they can help to develop work on tropical diseases in established laboratories of the United Kingdom and to associate this work with centres overseas where the diseases are endemic and the problems can be studied in patients. In addition to providing grants as at present, they may wish in due course to demonstrate a pattern of study by concentrating efforts on one such disease.

Veterinary Medicine and Animal Nutrition

Animals provide much of the protein foods consumed by man. From the standpoint of the welfare of man, study of the nutrition and diseases of animals is important. Work on animals is also relevant because comparative studies yield facts which assist the understanding of similar problems in man. Since veterinary medicine has lagged behind human medicine, advances can be expected from increased application of the principles and methods evolved for the latter. The trustees therefore intend to foster the development of research in this field, and, in particular, to promote more work on the tropical diseases of animals, since the need for protein foodstuffs is so much greater in the developing countries.

History of Medicine

The history of medicine was a special interest of Sir Henry Wellcome which the trustees will continue to support, believing that doctors and medical researchers should be better informed about the ways in which the great advances in knowledge, especially during the last century, have created the standards of medical practice and research which exist today. Their major expenditure in this field will continue to be on their Museum and Library in the Euston Road, and on the recently created Sub-Department of the History of Medicine at University College London. They hope that these centres will be a source of interest and inspiration to others in the development of medical history as a university subject.

Research Fellowships

The trustees at present award about 50 research fellowships each year. Some of these awards are competitive, such as those for clinical and veterinary research and the Sir Henry Wellcome Travelling Research Fellowships. But the majority are provided for graduates from overseas who wish to come to the United Kingdom to extend their research experience. The trustees believe that at present there is no shortage of fellowships for graduates of the United Kingdom who wish to undertake research in their own country.

The trustees intend for the future to provide fellowships of the following kinds:

a) Awards to encourage research in inadequately supported fields of medicine;

b) Competitive awards for graduates from a greater number of countries overseas who wish to extend their research experience by working in the United Kingdom. These competitive awards will gradually replace the present *ad hoc* fellowships. Some will be of senior status;

c) Awards to permit research workers in one field to obtain training in a second field and thus acquire interdisciplinary qualifications.

Communication between research workers in medicine

The trustees will continue their present policy which is designed to improve communications between research workers. They will therefore go on providing travel grants, support for symposia and small international meetings and grants to aid publication and illustration. They may also occasionally give help to medical research libraries and museums.

In the past the trustees have normally allocated most of the funds of the Trust on a short-term basis. In the future they intend to make a large part of the funds available in this way: but to undertake new developments on the lines now proposed it will be necessary sometimes to give longer-term support for projects which they wish to encourage. When the trustees assume such longer-term responsibilities they will work in close collaboration with the university or other institution concerned so that the project may always be closely linked with the development plans of the institution.

Up to the present, 45 per cent of the funds of the Wellcome Trust have been used to build research accommodation. The need for buildings is not likely to diminish, but the trustees consider it inappropriate as a policy that so large a proportion of their funds should continue to be used in this way. In order to make funds available to promote the objectives stated earlier the trustees will in future take a stricter view on requests for the provision of research accommodation and will normally consider them favourably only when a building proposed is to accommodate a programme of research which the trustees in any case desire to support. They take the view that, in general, laboratory space for research workers paid from public funds should be provided from public funds; its provision should not be dependent on a charitable foundation such as the Wellcome Trust.

In other respects the trustees will continue to make appropriate types of grants for the research programmes which they think should be supported.

In deciding on the new policy for research in 1966 the trustees were anxious to be independent from the Medical Research Council as their former links had created a view at the MRC that when they could not fit something into their budget they could just telephone the Trust. I remember once hearing McMichael say. "Isn't it splendid that the MRC now has funds available from the Trust to enable it to expand its activities." It was of course the case that the Trust had often provided funds for important MRC developments. A major grant for the equipping of the Laboratory of Molecular Biology in Cambridge comes to mind. We also built laboratories in Jamaica and The Gambia to house their Units and a floating Laboratory on the River Gambia, shades of the laboratory on the Nile provided by Henry Wellcome.

The Trust was very attached to the MRC and we admired the dynamism of its Secretary Sir Harold Himsworth who had developed it into such a significant supporter of Medical Research. To illustrate our relationship one only has to mention that Sir Henry Dale was Director of the National Institute for Medical Research for many years, McMichael and Thompson had been members of the Council, Boyd was a member of the Colonial Medical Research Committee, Green the Scientific Secretary of the Trust had been a Principal Medical Officer at the Headquarters of the Council for most of his working life and I had also been recruited from the Council. However we also believed that independence was important for the Trust so that it could stretch its ideas as it wished without any question of consulting the Council. The importance of this independence was illustrated some years later when the Chief Medical Officer at the Ministry of Health telephoned me to ask if the Trust would be willing to support a study of the sexual behavior of the British population as the data was required for the creation of a policy to control AI.DS. The proposal had been vetoed by the Prime Minister, Margaret Thatcher and £1 million was needed to pay for it. We made the grant which would have been impossible if we had been too closely linked to any government body.

The question that we had to answer was: what was the difference that we had to create, to justify being independent? One thing that I had noted when I was at the Council was that its structure depended on the character and ability of its Secretary. Himsworth was there for many years and had created its growth and form because of his personality and wide ranging interest in the whole subject. I suppose I wanted to do much the same at the Trust. The Council of the MRC was made up of representatives of the various disciplines and the appointments were for three years. I well remember one Council member who described the situation as follows: 'In the first year you were a new boy learning the ropes. In the second you could formulate and plan what you thought needed to be done for your subject and put it before the Council. If supported it would begin to receive action but that was your last year and you could not foster it thereafter and so it might be negated by your subject successor who would have his own ideas and in any case you would not be involved.'

At the Trust the situation was different. What we had was a continuing team. The scientific trustees held their appointments until they reached the age of 67. There was therefore the possibility of following through initiatives without having to pass them over. This was potentially a mixed blessing because the organisation could become stagnated and that was precisely what had happened in its early years when there was no retirement age. Dale stayed on until he was 87 and Boyd until he was 75 and the secretariat had very little room for taking an initiative. When I took over there were three scientists who were keen to make changes and we were together for a number of years. The scientific staff of the Trust was also there for a number of years and worked directly with the Trustees in the clinical, basic science and tropical programmes. We were all able to make our input and together this became the policy. I remember our first financial officer saying to me that it was a bad method of management because any one of the staff might use his direct contact with a trustee to undermine my authority. I never experienced such a danger I suppose because we had all become such good friends and members of a team.

The members of the board that I worked with stayed together for about ten years and then were replaced as they retired. The number had been increased to seven, and the staff also grew. The new scientific members were Gordon Smith , Dean of the London School of Hygiene and Tropical Medicine, Stanley Peart Professor of Medicine at St Mary's Hospital, William Paton, Professor of Pharmacology at Oxford, Helen Muir, Director of the Kennedy Institute of Rheumatology. Others followed but by that time the cohesive structure had broken up because of its size. Nevertheless, especially in the case of Stanley Peart the initiatives in mental health, ophthalmology and dermatology took off and Robert Thompson was a wise head in the veterinary and biochemical fields. We were able to keep the same pattern of working until about 1986. When I interviewed Helen Muir about her time at the Trust she drew my attention to the difficulty experienced by a new Trustee joining the very close-knit club that had come into being.

Having decided on the board's new policy it was necessary to make arrangements to implement it. A transfer to the support of individuals meant that we would be open to the receipt of many more applications which would have to be processed and peer reviewed. Fellowships would need to be advertised, short-listed and meetings organised for interviews and all of these things would make it necessary to have more space and staff.

Dr Edda Hanington had joined me in 1965 and had learned rapidly how to manage the grant system. In 1967 Ben Bembridge and Tom Hopwood were added and the subject areas in the policy were divided between us. Everyone had to learn how to process grant applications and this was helped by the recruitment of Maurice Barren and Derek Metcalfe both of whom had worked in the MRC. The Clinical and Veterinary side were run by Edda, Basic Science and overseas fellowships by Ben and Tropical by Tom. I kept up an interest in the tropical programme and also looked after the history of medicine. As time passed these early staff were replaced by Michael Morgan a biochemist, Lawrence Smaje, physiology, David Gordon clinical, Keith Sinclair veterinary, James Howard and Bridget Ogilvie tropical. The programme in the history of medicine was run by Rupert Hall and Harold Edwards fostered the Senior Fellowships.

Panels usually under the chairmanship of a trustee were appointed to judge the applications. These panels had the following areas of interest: Infection and Immunity, Physiology and Pharmacology, Molecular and Cell, Mental Health and Neurosciences, Vision Research, Clinical Interest Group, Veterinary, Tropical Interest Group and History of Medicine. The trustees enjoyed chairing these panels because they were covering subjects in which they had a personal interest.

The following two tables illustrate the effect of these policy decisions.

Table 1 shows the transfer of emphasis to the support of projects in place of buildings and equipment:

Table 1 The financial consequence of the new policy (1966) on grants for buildings and equipment

Year	Buildings	Equipment	Total Funds Available		
	£	£	£		
1937-56	322,000	52,000	374,000	= 51% of	740,000
1956-8*	544,000	171,000	715,000	= 69% of	1,060,000
1958-60	612,000	163,000	775,000	= 65% of	1,200,000
1960-2	883,000	432,000	1,315,000	= 66% of	2,000,000
1962-4	785,000	428,000	1,213,000	= 61% of	2,000,000
1964-6	946,000	288,000	1,234,000	= 46% of	2,670,000
1966-8	429,000	363,000	792,000	= 28% of	2,780,000
1968-70	406,000	348,000	754,000	= 13% of	5,780,000
1970-2	36,000	206,000	242,000	= 5% of	4,840,000
1972-4	23,000	180,000	203,000	= 4% of	4,479,000
1974-6	138,000	293,000	431,000	= 6% of	7,240,000

*Biennial totals

Table 2 shows the increase in expenditure on grants for research and expenses. What is not shown is the percentage of awards that were being made for the support of individuals on fellowships of one type or another.

Table 2 Awards for Research Assistance and Expenses in Basic and Clinical Sciences

	£		£
1937-56	40,000	= 5% of total expenditure	740,000
1956-8	65,000	= 6% of total expenditure	1,060,000
1958-60	98,000	= 8% of total expenditure	1,200,000
1960-2	140,000	= 7% of total expenditure	2,000,000
1962-4	149,000	= 7% of total expenditure	2, 000,000
1964-6	244,000	= 9% of total expenditure	2,670,000
1966-8	961,000	= 34% of total expenditure	2,780,000
1968-70	2,033,000	= 35% of total expenditure	5,780,000
1970-2	1,307,000	= 27% of total expenditure	4,844,000
1972-4	1,133,000	= 25% of total expenditure	4,479,000
1974-6	2,501,000	= 34% of total expenditure	7,240,000
1976-8	3,183,000	= 26% of total expenditure	12,369,000
1978-80	5,142,000	= 25% of total expenditure	20,672,000
1980-2	6,118,000	= 25% of total expenditure	24,500,000
1982-4	7,671,000	= 21% of total expenditure	35,842,000
TOTAL	**31,000,000**	(approx.)	**128,000,0000**

The last column of the table shows the biennial growth of the Trust's expenditure. Stated on an annual basis these figures are £530,000 in 1956 to £1,890,000 in 1966, to £6,184,500 in 1976 and £17,921,000 in 1984 (not adjusted for inflation). Most of this growth had occurred in the last three years. Figures from the accounts of the Company show 1967 income as £1.5m, 1976 as £3.7m and 1985 as £23.8m.

In 1986 the Trust celebrated its fiftieth anniversary and its history was written by Hall and Bembridge and published as *Physic and Philanthropy*. The twenty years between the publication of the policy statement and the 50th anniversary of the Trust were admirably analysed.

The Queen and Duke of Edinburgh attended a soirée in the Wellcome Building on the 4th of December for which many demonstrations of the Trust's work had been prepared. During the year ten universities put on exhibitions of the Trust's support. There were also meetings arranged by societies which illustrated the contribution to their subject field.

In summary I would describe our achievements as follows: We increased the funds available to medical research to such an extent that by 1996 the budget was similar to that of the MRC. As a consequence there were many more people working on medical research mainly in the universities. The influence of their presence on the quality of medicine was therefore very significant. This also meant that Britain a relatively small country was able to continue to be a leader in the field in which it had earlier done so much pioneering work. More particularly because of the Trust's scientifically based structure and freedom it had a significant influence in certain fields which we had identified as inadequately supported e.g. mental health, dermatology, ophthalmic medicine, the health of animals and tropical medicine. Because of our interest in basic science we had been able to foster projects in new areas long before they had become established. Molecular biology was one of these which led on to our later input into research on mapping the human genome. We had taken an early interest in Nuclear Magnetic Resonance before it was scaled up for use in clinical medicine. This broad coverage meant that we were able to recognise the advantage from interdisciplinary studies so as to encourage the application of basic sciences to clinical specialties. Our international remit had been important in encouraging links with research overseas and especially the tropics Because we were not inhibited by political barriers, we had an international influence for example in WHO. Our activities in tropical medicine and the history of medicine are described in more detail because the Trust had a continuity of interest in them stemming from Henry Wellcome.

The period from 1987 to 1991, when I retired, was the beginning of something very different because, on account of the sale of Wellcome shares, and the shrewd investment of the money raised from the sale the funds available had grown so rapidly. I think those years should be more appropriately described together with the events up to the present day. In any case I would find it difficult to write such an account myself since one of the effects of growth was to make me more remote from the science we were supporting. Bridget Ogilvie became Director of Scientific Programmes and I became more involved in the reconstruction of the Wellcome Building and the plans for the future of the much enlarged Trust.

I had found the time when we were a small cohesive group excited by the science we were supporting much more in tune with my temperament. I expect this is quite a common experience among people who are in charge of any organisation that grows from rags to riches.

Sir John McMichael

Sir John McMichael was the Professor of Medicine at the Royal Postgraduate Medical School at Hammersmith and probably the leading academic figure in medicine in this country. A physiologist by training, he had for many years been in his position at Hammersmith and created there the leading clinical research institution in Britain. He was a very busy man but placed the activities of the Trust very high on his agenda. He was always willing to help in whatever way was needed. He had a considerable personal interest in the welfare of young people entering clinical research and was willing to attend to such personal detail as the applications for travel grants.

His greatest contribution to the Trust was his strong belief in clinical science after the period of basic science under Henry Dale. His tremendous knowledge of the people of research from all over the Commonwealth, was a significant factor in the breadth of the trustees' operations at that time. The Royal Postgraduate Medical School in the immediate post-war years was the Mecca for up and coming physicians and surgeons from the old Commonwealth. When these people returned home, they set up research units which required support and the Trust was, therefore with good knowledge, able to give considerable grants for research in New Zealand, Australia, South Africa and Canada. The applications from these places diminished when these graduates had retired and the focus of postgraduate training for the Commonwealth turned towards the United States. The Postgraduate Medical School was the recipient of many large grants during this time. I have no doubt that this was due to their pre-eminence in research and not to special pleading by Sir John McMichael. I came to know the people there extremely well and regularly attended their postgraduate teaching rounds.

He was a quite exceptional man and brought to the Trust two schemes that have survived the test of time. The first, the Senior Research Fellowships in Clinical Science and the second, the Anglo-Swedish exchange fellowships. For the former, McMichael had recognised the problem of young doctors in their early thirties who were anxious to get on with their research but for whom there was no suitable post to bridge them between the early years and those of senior academic appointments. These Fellowships, two (and later more) a year, established the careers of many of future leaders of clinical research

The Swedish Fellowships also fulfilled a need. Sweden at that time was very advanced in medico-physiological research and it was the natural place for many young people to spend a year. The two-way scheme with the Swedish Medical Research Council was extremely helpful.

Professor Robert Thompson

I first met Robert Thompson when he was appointed to the Council of the MRC during the time that I was working there. I had to go through the applications for grants with him as he was chairman of the Appointments and Grants Committee. I was delighted when the Trustees decided to appoint him to a vacancy at the Trust.

He became a trustee in 1963, when he held the Chair of Chemical Pathology at Guy's Hospital Medical School. Not long afterwards, in 1965, he succeeded Sir Charles Dodds as head of the Courtauld Institute of Biochemistry at the Middlesex Hospital Medical School. The trustees decided that they needed to have a biochemist on the board because at that time the biochemical aspects of nearly all applications were a dominant feature. We needed expert advice and we got it in a quiet unassuming way. Robert, a man of immense charm balanced his science with a sophisticated view of life which made him an excellent companion.

We travelled to East Africa and South America together and always found great humour in all we saw. He was a strong supporter of new ideas for development and so I could rely on his backing. He took a considerable interest in the work of the Veterinary Panel and was its chairman for many years. There were, maybe, two negative aspects of his trusteeship. In the first place, he was against the creation of basic science fellowships, equivalent to the ones in clinical science created by John McMichael. I think he felt that other opportunities were available and that they were not necessary. Later on, when we

Henry with his parents Solomon and Mary Wellcome, and brother George (behind father) in 1869.

Log-cabin school at Garden City.

Wellcome in canoeing attire.

Syrie Wellcome, 1902.

Silas Burroughs.

Sir Henry (seated) with Thomas Nevin and George Pearson in America 1935.

One of the last photographs taken of
Sir Henry Wellcome.

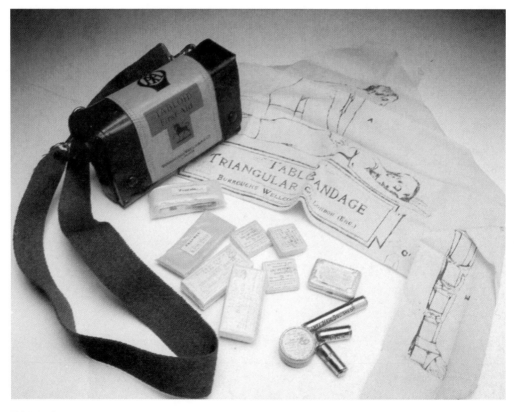

Tabloid first aid kit for the AA.

Sir Henry M. Stanley (1841–1904),
the famous explorer and friend of
Wellcome.

Floating laboratory on the Nile (1907).

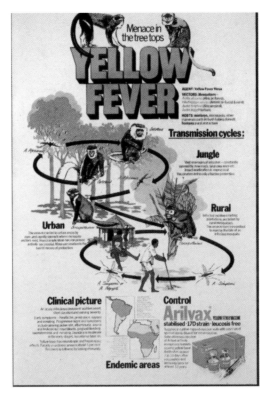

Poster advertising the need to vaccinate against Yellow Fever.

Her Majesty the Queen and His Royal Highness Prince Philip signing the visitor's book in the presence of Sir David Steel and Mr. A.J. Shepperd. (1987)

Trustees and staff at a presentation luncheon for the Nobel Laureates Dr. George Hitchings and Dr Gertrude Elion.
L to R: Dr. Julian Jack, Sir Roger Gibbs, Mrs. Hitchings, Dr. Bridget Ogilvie, Dr. George Hitchings, Dr. James Howard, Dr. Howard Schaeffer, Lord Swann, Sir David Steel, Lord Franks, US Company President, Dr. Gertrude Elion, Sir Stanley Peart, Professor Robert Thompson, Dr. Peter Williams, Dr. Helen Muir, Mr. Ian McGregor, Mr.Derek Metcalfe.

The Wellcome Building, 183 Euston Road, London NW1.

Signing the formal documents allowing the floatation of Wellcome Plc.
L to R: Dr. Gordon Smith, Sir David Steel, Mr. Russell Denoon-Duncan, Mr. Lawrence Banks.

The Board of Trustees in 1962
L to R: Sir Henry Dale, Sir John Boyd, Sir John McMichael, Dr. Frank Green, Lord Piercy, Dr. Peter Williams, Mr. Martin Price, Mr. Robert Nesbitt, Mr. Jack Clarke.

Lord Franks.

The Trustees and Director during a visit to the Burroughs Wellcome manufacturing plant in Greenville, North Carolina, in 1986.
L to R: Dr. Peter Williams, Sir Stanley Peart, Dr. Helen Muir, Sir David Steel, Dr. Gordon Smith, Dr. Julian Jack, US Director of Production.

Peter Williams in his office with applications
for consideration during one month.

Sir Henry Hallett Dale, O.M., G.B.E., M.D., P.R.S.
1875–1968.

Two Nobel Prize winners, Sir John Vane Director of
Group Research and Development making a
presentation to Dr. George Hitchings on his
retirement.

The Trust Offices, 1 Park Square West, London.

Burroughs Wellcome Headquarters, Research Triangle Park, Raleigh, North Carolina.

Wellcome Foundation Laboratories, Beckenham, Kent.

The Lady Dale floating laboratory at the Medical
Research Council Laboratories in the Gambia
(1959) and Gambian stamps.

Wellcome parasitology field laboratory in Ethiopia (1970).

Sir John McMichael, Dr. Peter Williams and Dr. Billie Williams (1975).

The reading Room of the Wellcome Library for the History of Medicine in 1982.

Professor Robert Thompson 1972 (Trustee).

Lord Franks presents Mr. Alfred Shepperd with a gift to commemorate the 100th Anniversary of the Wellcome Foundation (1980).

Dr. Tom Hopwood (Assistant Director of the Trust with responsibility for Tropical Medicine).

Sir Roger Gibbs.

Edda Hanington, Deputy Director of the Trust 1975

Administrative Headquarters of UK and Ireland zone at Crewe, Cheshire.

established such a scheme, I think that our experience showed that it might have been worth while to have done it earlier.

He was a classical chemical pathologist and found it difficult to come to grips with the way in which molecular biology was taking over. The MRC had played a pioneering role in this field and so we left it to them. It soon became obvious that molecular biology was becoming central to much of biochemistry and could do with more support than the MRC could provide and so the Trust did more in this field after Robert Thompson's retirement.

Dr Edda Hanington

I first met Edda in 1954 when I was the medical specialist at the British Military Hospital at Iserlohn in Germany. She came there as the wife of John Hanington who was the Obstetrics and Gynaecology specialist at the Hospital.

In 1965, Edda came to see me really to explore what she might do now that her children were at school and she wanted to get back to work. It so happened that I was at that stage needing to get someone to help me at the Trust with our medico-scientific activities and so, after consultation with the trustees, and an interview, she was appointed Assistant Scientific Secretary. One point from the interview that Edda always remembered was that she was asked by Sir John Boyd if she could type, which suggested that his recognition that women could be qualified in medicine was relatively small. She could not type but, nevertheless, got the job.

Edda's experience of medicine was the background that she provided at the Trust. What was special about her was that she was not satisfied to limit herself to the routine and began to think how she might promote research in areas of special interest to her. These areas turned out to be mental health, dermatology and migraine. I am bound to say in parentheses that this interest had been stimulated by problems in her family in these areas of medicine, an interesting piece of history on why the Trust should have selected these special topics for research support. However, it is not enough to indicate areas because they concern you. You have then to show that something can be done about them if you develop a programme and provide special support. She convinced the trustees and so a Mental Health Panel was appointed to try and bridge the gap between the people who studied the brain and the world of psychiatry which was much more orientated towards psychoanalysis. Fellowships were started and recruits to the field were gathered. Edda played a special role in looking after these protégés and encouraging them when their spirit weakened. There was always one or other of them in her office telling her not only of their research but of their family affairs as well. She became to some extent a mother to these new recruits to this field.

Edda then turned to dermatology, another subject in which there was a dearth of research. The chief opportunity lay with the support of Professor Sam Shuster who was a general physician who had been appointed to the Chair of Dermatology at Newcastle. He set about creating an academic department. The Trust provided funds for a building and some appointments. Shuster gathered around him people with the same urge as he had himself. From that department the people he trained went on to head academic dermatology departments at the Institute of Dermatology in London and at Cardiff. The initiative was very productive.

Her third subject interest was in migraine. She became fascinated by the headache and raised blood pressure produced when people with depression took mono-amine-oxidase-inhibitors and ate certain cheeses. She remembered that sufferers from migraine often insisted that certain dietary factors such as chocolate and cheese and red wine precipitated an attack of migraine. She wondered if there might be a link. To study this she collected a group of patients and controls who said that they suffered from dietary migraine. She then ran, from the office, a double blind trial in which she gave each group at random a tablet containing tyramine or lactose. I remember well the excitement as we waited for the post to come in to find out whether these people had an attack of migraine and then to discover whether they had been taking lactose or tyramine. The results were almost 100% in favour of tyramine as a precipitating factor of migraine. Edda went on to more extensive studies in this field, which proved unequivocally that some cases of migraine were precipitated by amines. She began work in a migraine clinic on one day a week and wrote a book on the subject. This example of originality developing in someone undertaking the administration of research gave me enormous pleasure as it illustrated the type of person that I felt could best administer the programme of scientific research at the Trust.

In Edda Hanington we had a strange mixture: a somewhat self-effacing, maternal woman, with a concern for those for whom she was responsible, conscientiousness in undertaking her work but also with the vision to perceive an original idea and develop it to fruition. She was a great recruit to the Trust although my reasons for recruiting her were somewhat tenuous.

Dr Ben Bembridge

Ben Bembridge got to know about the possibility of a job at the Trust because his brother-in-law, Professor David Mollin, whom I knew very well, recommended him.

He was an ophthalmologist in Edinburgh who had shown considerable enterprise in his earlier years in undertaking research with Dr Antoinette Pirie in Oxford. He was also a man of interesting depth of learning, for instance, he was an authority on the early Jesuit missionaries in China. On the other hand, he was a very quiet, retiring, man and this kind of information only came out after years of acquaintanceship.

Ben worked very conscientiously at the Trust, handling the basic science side of the Grants Programme and the development of fellowships for scientists from all parts of Europe. He also took a special interest in the development of the links between ophthalmology and medicine, which we were anxious to promote. After he retired from the Trust, he put a lot of effort into writing the scientific part of the History of the Trust, the other part of which came from the pen of Professor Rupert Hall.

His contribution to the development of basic sciences in the universities was much more important than anyone realised.

CHAPTER 7

Tropical Medicine

I doubt whether many people would think of tropical medicine as a central purpose of a medical research charity in Britain. However if they knew something of Henry Wellcome's life they would not be surprised. As I have said earlier his introduction to the tropics was through his friendship with Henry Morton Stanley. In 1901 he visited the Sudan on the advice of his doctors following a bout of pneumonia. He found the climate in Khartoum delightful and he made a rapid recovery. It was the first time that he had visited the tropics and been able to observe the tremendous difference between the comfort of the governing classes and the native population. He met Lord Kitchener and visited the unfinished Gordon Memorial College which had been built using a donation of £123,000 collected in the City of London. He was struck by the fact that no provision had been made for scientific research laboratories. He felt that 'if a man could work there under such favourable conditions and yet had all the elements for research at his finger-ends it would be a great advantage'. He offered to build and equip laboratories and to find a team to work in them. His offer was accepted and the governing body of the College undertook the payment of the staff and running costs. He visited the Sudan many times during the next few years and also financed and took part in major archaeological excavations.

Wellcome appointed Dr Andrew Balfour to run these laboratories and a little later he was joined by C M Wenyon who operated from a floating laboratory in a Nile houseboat which Wellcome provided so that he could work further afield.

This was the start of Wellcome's involvement in tropical medicine. He took a great personal interest in Balfour's work and arranged for lavish reports to be published. A full account of the work is described by Len Goodwin and E Beveridge in *Wellcome's Legacies*. The staff had risen from two when he started to nine when he left in 1913 on account of his health. It was said that: "His influence on living conditions in Khartoum, which he had transformed into a modern city, and on the public health and medical services of the country, had been immense."

When Balfour returned to London in 1913 Wellcome created the Wellcome Bureau of Scientific Research and made Balfour the Director in Chief. This position not only made him responsible for the laboratories of tropical medicine and Wellcome's historical museum but also meant that Frederick Power, who was Wellcome's chief scientific lieutenant, and Henry Dale, Director of his Physiological Research Laboratories, were under his direction. Both of them left within the year

Balfour also established the Wellcome Museum of Medical Science based on his own collections and this came to be a very important teaching aid for students of the subject from the neighbouring London School of Tropical Medicine. Doctors from the armed services and the Colonial Service used to visit the museum to learn about tropical medicine before they took up their overseas postings. There was no point in moving this museum to Beckenham in 1965 when the laboratories were relocated there, so it was transferred to the care of the Trust.

The laboratories thrived for 52 years and their activities together with those of the Historical Museum and the Wellcome Museum of Medical Science became Wellcome's central interest. In 1934 he built the Wellcome Building in the Euston Road to house them.

The Laboratories of the Bureau were involved in the First World War soon after they were established. Balfour was given the rank of lieutenant-colonel and became President of the Medical Advisory Committee of the Mediterranean Expeditionary Force. He and his staff operated in Salonika, Egypt, Mesopotamia, India and Palestine. When the war was over the Bureau was reopened in London and laboratories were acquired for it in 1920 in Endsleigh Gardens. In 1923 Balfour became the Director of the London School of Hygiene and Tropical Medicine nearby in Mallet Street and was knighted. Wenyon was appointed Director in Chief and occupied the post until he retired in 1944 when Charles Kellaway followed. Kellaway made great strides in rationalising the research activities of the Wellcome Company, among which was the amalgamation of the tropical programme of the Wellcome Bureau with the Wellcome Chemical Research Laboratories. The new entity was called the Wellcome Laboratories of Tropical Medicine and now included a therapeutic purpose of interest to the Company.

Sir John Boyd was appointed director and under him the laboratory continued with its fundamental research on Trypanosomes (Cecil Hoare), Leptospirosis (Broom, who had been made an OBE for his work on Yellow Fever during the war) and viral biochemistry (John Bauer). The chemists were developing compounds for the treatment of trypanosomiasis and babesia. It was at this time that the antimalarial Daraprim which had been synthesised in the New York laboratories was tested on the malarial screens developed by Len Goodwin. Bauer at this stage found that a thiosemicarbazone also from New York was effective against the Smallpox virus. It was marketed as Marboran but was not needed because of the success of the World Health Organisation's programme which eradicated Smallpox. Later Bauer played an important part in showing the effectiveness of Schaeffer's antiviral Zovirax against the Herpes virus. Compounds for the treatment of Helminthic diseases (worms) in man and animals were also made and tested.

The laboratories celebrated their 50th anniversary in 1963 but were transferred to Beckenham in 1965 and gradually ceased to be a special entity as the Company did not think there was a profitable market for drugs to treat parasitic infections in the tropics.

The Wellcome Trust's Support for Tropical Medicine

In his will, Wellcome specifically stipulated the support for tropical medical research. No doubt he thought it would operate alongside his tropical laboratories, but he had not envisaged that by creating the Wellcome Foundation he had left the laboratories to the business and therefore outside the trustees' purview. Sir John Boyd, who had been director of the laboratories, became a trustee in 1955. The Trust was still too impecunious to consider financing a revival of the Tropical Laboratories outside the Company but I find it hard to believe that it did not cross his mind.

The Trust's first grant in the field of tropical medicine was made in 1945 when it endowed the Wellcome Professorship of Clinical Tropical Medicine at the London School of Hygiene and Tropical Medicine.

When I joined the staff the only two tropical activities of the Trust were the support of Doctors Henry Foy and Athena Kondi in Nairobi working on anaemia and hookworm in Kenya, and Dr Selwyn Baker, an Australian missionary working on sprue at the Christian Medical College in Vellore, South India.

The 1960s could not have been a more appropriate time to support research in this field. The opportunity for a post in tropical medicine and facilities in the tropics was about to experience a catastrophic decline because of the granting of independence to the former colonies of the European metropolitan powers. It is not often realised that progress in the treatment of tropical diseases was often due to the doctors who were need-ed to live and work in the tropics to look after the health of the Colonial Civil Servants or in India the military and probably their servants. These doctors observed the diseases of the local population and began to consid-er their cause since that had not featured in their training. Very few medi-cines, other than quinine for malaria, were active against these diseases. It soon became apparent that these were new diseases to European eyes. They had various native names but when their nature was understood their names became Latinized e.g. onchercerciasis (river blindness), Leishmaniasis (Leishmann was a Scottish doctor), and filariasis. Few ordi-nary mortals understood what the doctors were talking about especially when one realizes that they were of various nationalities working in many different countries and using their own languages to name the diseases. The Director of the National Institute for the Blind was able to raise much more interest and money when he called the disease in West Africa River Blindness instead of Onchercerciasis!

One of the earliest of these discoveries was made by Patrick Manson in Amoy, China when he was in the employ of the Customs service. He showed that a sandfly transmitted a filarial worm to one of his patients. This discovery that parasites could be transmitted through the bite of an insect completely changed the understanding of many diseases and even more so when Ronald Ross, in India, showed that bird malaria could be transmitted by an anopheline mosquito.

From then on all over the world doctors and zoologists were seeking the cause and transmission of the parasites of many tropical diseases. Research laboratories were built in India and a School of Tropical Medicine in Calcutta. An Institute of Medical Research was built in Kuala Lumpur, Malaysia and schools of Tropical Medicine were founded at the turn of the century in Liverpool and London to train doctors who were going to work in the Colonies. There were other such university schools in Paris, Hamburg and Rome. A Colonial Medical Research Service was created.

India was in the forefront of research but, when it became independent in 1947, the expatriates left and the emphasis on research was transferred in part to East and West Africa.

When I was working at the MRC between 1955 and 1960 I listed the following places where there were research establishments:

Table 3 A list of the activities in tropical medicine in which the MRC and the Colonial Medical Research Committee had an interest in 1956

CAMEROONS	Helminthiasis Research Unit, Kumba – Loaiasis and Onchercerciasis.
GAMBIA MRC	Laboratories, Fajara: – Malaria, Sickle cell anaemia, Anaemia, Bilharzia.
GOLD COAST	Bolgatanga – Onchocerciasis: Kumasi – Tuberculosis: Accra – Morbid Anatomy (Eddington) – Diabetes and Hypertension (Dodu) – Sickle cell anaemia in pregnancy (Bannerman).
NIGERIA	Lagos, Virus Research Institute, Yellow Fever, Poliomyelitis, Zika, West Nile viruses: Ibadan, Nutrition, Guinea worm, West Sokoto, Malaria Control Project, Central laboratories: Nigerian Leprosy Service.
KENYA	Nairobi, Sand flies, Division of Insect Borne Diseases – Kala-Azar; Tuberculosis Chemotherapy trials; Kerngoya, Relapsing Fever RU.
UGANDA	Makerere: MRC Group for research on Infantile Malnutrition, Entebbe, East African Virus Research Institute, Various Arbor viruses and their vectors.
TANGANYIKA	Amani, East African Institute of Malaria and vector-borne diseases, Mwanza, Schistosomiasis, Filariasis: Taveta-Pare, Malaria control project.
JAMAICA	University of the West Indies, MRC Tropical Metabolism Research Unit, Various projects by the staff on for example Ackee poisoning.
TRINIDAD	Port-of-Spain, Trinidad Regional Virus Laboratory, in the Rockerfeller Foundation Laboratory in St Clair.
MALAYA	Kuala Lumpur, Institute for Medical Research, Leprosy, Scrub Typhus, Filariasis, Virus research, Japanese encephalitis
JORDAN	Trachoma Research Unit.

Only two of these, the MRC laboratories at Fajara in The Gambia, and the Tropical Metabolism Research Unit in Jamaica, remained ten years later, and there was no Colonial Research Service to provide jobs for a new generation to work in the tropics. There was however one new development outside the colonial system: the creation of Universities in Ibadan (Nigeria), Kampala (Uganda) and Kingston (Jamaica). These universities were at first staffed by expatriates and so for a few years attracted the future generation of tropical researchers. The medical staff of the universities had experience of temperate diseases not endemic tropical diseases and so, with the encouragement of Himsworth, who had a similar background, they started to work on the way in which, say, diabetes, malnutrition, hypertension and cancer behaved in the tropical setting. Eldryd Parry was one of these new recruits and after a spell at Ibadan and Addis Ababa established a department at Zaria in Northern Nigeria, to which he recruited David Warrell and Anthony Bryceson and others who would go on to play an important part in the future development of medical research in the tropics. In Jamaica Waterlow, Champ Alleyne and David Picou were later joined by Alan Jackson and Mike Golden. The last three in turn took charge of the unit when Waterlow returned to London. A new discipline came into being – 'Medicine in the Tropics' and this created a very fertile field which involved doctors from Europe and America and created a stimulus for the subject. This concept enabled the medical Trustees to feel included in the tropical programme and Robert Thompson became involved in a study of neurological disease in Cassava eaters in Nigeria. Stanley Peart also saw the opportunity to study why the incidence of hypertension in the population of Kenya increased in those who migrated from the country villages to work in the towns.

The progress of the research in the tropical units was of particular interest because it had continuity and all the costs were provided by the Trust. Over the years the office staff got to know the researchers, had regular reports on their progress and made frequent visits. Also the trustees were willing to go to see the work and pay visits to some unusual locations where we would also see the people at the local branches of the Wellcome Foundation.

The Nairobi unit was working on malnutrition and anaemia. They had established a baboon colony for their studies. When Foy and Kondi retired the work turned to the parasitic disease Schistosomiasis, called Bill Harris by the British troops after its other name Bilharziaiasis. The studies on immunity to the parasite were very fruitful. Later the operation moved to Kilifi on the coast where its staff studied Malaria. This unit, now much expanded, is still very active.

The Kilifi operation was linked to the Nuffield department of medicine in Oxford as was another unit in Bangkok which was established under David Warrell. He worked on cerebral malaria and venomous snakes and his wife Mary studied rabies. After they left, the unit was taken over by Nick White who extended it into Vietnam and it now occupies a leading international role in malarial studies. He was recently made an F R S.

Another activity was the study of sprue. This disease causes patients to get chronic fatty diarrhoea which makes the sufferers very thin and deficient in Vitamin B12, the lack of which causes megaloblastic (large celled) anaemia. The objective was to find the cause, and to do this we mounted a study to compare sprue and megaloblastic anaemia in patients in Vellore, Hammersmith, London, Nairobi, Singapore in the Army, and Haiti. A book about the results was published by the Trust.

An early Unit was established in Belem at the mouth of the Amazon under Ralph Lainson and Jeffrey Shaw. They were based in the Rockefeller arbor virus unit in the Evandro Chagas Institute. They worked on a parasitic disease called espundia which causes disfiguring, destructive facial sores. Lainson isolated the parasite and identified the sand fly that transmitted it from the reservoir in forest rodents. For this work he was made a Fellow of the Royal Society. It reminded me of the pioneering stories that had so enthralled me as a student.

Bill Bray set up a unit in Ethiopia and discovered the reservoir of the local form of Leishmaniasis.

In Kingston, Jamaica at the University of the West Indies we took over support of the MRC. Tropical Metabolism Unit when the Council ceased to fund it. Mike Golden did stalwart work there on various aspects of protein malnutrition. Also in Jamaica we built a laboratory for epidemiological research which subsequently was the base for the Sickle Cell Disease Unit under Graham Sergeant.

In the Gambia we provided accommodation for the Trachoma Unit and a floating laboratory in an elegant river boat. Dr Sowa in the Trachoma unit isolated the trachoma virus which had earlier been found by a Dr Chang in China. This was the first isolation of the cause outside China and led on to great improvement in the treatment of this blinding disease so prevalent in many of the poorer regions of the world. The floating laboratory turned out to be too great a strain on the unit's financial resources and so was used very little.

We were also giving a lot of support to the Schools of Tropical Medicine in London and Liverpool. One of our objectives was to have all our overseas units linked to home bases and an important one of these was Professor David Weatherall's Nuffield Department of Medicine in Oxford. He was always a stalwart supporter of the tropical programme and later became a trustee. These home bases gave the tropical researchers some stability and links to new research ideas.

All of these activities were open to threats of violence. In Jamaica the campus was terrorised by vagabonds from the hills behind. In Nigeria the campus became dangerous and the coastal unit in Kenya was insecure. Addis Ababa became untenable. But this element did not destroy what we were doing.

At one stage I became very involved with encouraging the World Health Organisation to embark upon tropical research and the Tropical Diseases Research programme funded by many countries was developed and supported a lot of research. I also set up a research project to link the Harvard School of Tropical Public Health to the London School of Tropical Medicine. Both institutions created fellowships to work in Brazil and the London School sponsored Mike Golden who went to Jamaica. The Schools never worked together partly because of the different terms of service for nationals of America and Britain.

At about the time of my retirement I initiated, with my wife Billie a book of essays entitled *The Wellcome Illustrated History of Tropical Diseases*. Frank Cox supported by Rosemary Tilden took over the editorship and brought it to publication. Billie also made films on the History of Sleeping Sickness. I wrote about some of the lighter episodes of our activities in tropical medicine and published them in my autobiography, *The Exotic Fruits of my Life*. The Trust has continued and expanded its tropical research activities since I retired.

I wish now to pay a special tribute to Len Goodwin, who spent most of his working life in the Wellcome Foundation and in 1955, became Director of the Wellcome Laboratory of Tropical Medicine (WLTM). He was appointed Director of Research at the London Zoo in 1964 just before the laboratories moved to Beckenham. I had got to know him well when he was Director of the WLTM and met him frequently to talk about the future of tropical research and how the Trust could help. More practically he and his wife Marie gave a home base to the Laboratories in Nairobi after Foy and Kondi retired. When Len retired he took charge of the Wellcome Museum of Medical Science when Tony Duggan the Director decided to resign. He revived its work on audio visual presentation of the resources of the museum and directed it until it had to be closed down for the reconstruction of the Wellcome Building. With Elizabeth Beveridge he wrote the story in *Wellcome Legacies, Sir Henry Wellcome and Tropical Medicine*. In retirement he researched the story of Silas Burroughs the co-founder of Burroughs Wellcome and Co and showed his great significance to all that followed after he died. Len was as cheerful as ever when I spoke to him in October 2008 but I have just heard that he died in November at the age of 93. In all these developments Gordon Smith, the Dean of the London School of Tropical Medicine, who became a trustee in 1972, Tom Hopwood and later Bridget Ogilvie, who succeeded me as director of the Trust, played important roles.

Dr Gordon Smith

It is somewhat difficult for me to write an account of Gordon Smith's trusteeship because we became great personal friends and played golf together regularly during the last five or six years of his life.

I first knew him when he had recently returned from Malaya to a lectureship at the London School of Hygiene. He was obviously very enthusiastic to do something new for tropical medicine against the background of what he called the world of the dinosaurs! Despite this outspokenness, he was much admired by his colleagues and supported particularly by Dr Raymond Lewthwaite, the then Chief Medical Research Adviser to the Colonial Office. Lewthwaite had been Gordon's Director at the Institute for Medical Research in Kuala Lumpur. Gordon did not, however, come into the orbit of the Trust at that time. From the School he went to be Director of Porton, the Micro-biological Research establishment of the Ministry of Defence. In this position he had a very high profile as there was a considerable amount of anti-biological warfare campaigning going on. After he had been there a while, either he fell out with them or he decided that the time had come to move on and he accepted the position of Dean of the London School of Hygiene.

The Trustees at about this time needed an adviser on tropical matters as Sir John Boyd had retired. Gordon was the obvious choice since he did not come from any of the tropical establishments but had all the right credentials. He was recruited in the first place as a Scientific Adviser and became a trustee when the number was increased from five to seven

Gordon had a tendency, when chairing the Tropical Panel, to introduce the next item by saying, "This is a totally useless application, do we need to speak about it?" Or "When in doubt throw it out" which did not give much room for the members of the Panel to express their opinions.

Gordon was devoted to the Trust, had become somewhat bored with the Deanship of the School and would very much like to have taken charge of the Trust but had to hold back because of its structure. During his last year when he was already suffering his terminal illness, he put in tremendous efforts to see that the trustees considered carefully the appointment of my successor. He would have so liked to have taken on the job himself and I have often speculated how the Trust would have developed if he was Deputy Chairman when Bridget Ogilvie took over!

I loved him truly and have written elsewhere of our friendship.

Dr Tom Hopwood

Tom Hopwood was recruited when he was Medical Adviser to the Department of Health in Ethiopia. His background was that he had entered the Colonial Service after qualifying, worked for a number of years in the Falkland Islands, and then, after a period in more junior posts, became the Deputy Director of Medical Services in Uganda. He had a considerable insight into tropical medicine in East Africa and an acquaintanceship with most of the people in the field. Immediately before he went to Ethiopia, he had been on the staff of the MRC so he knew something of the medical research grant-giving business.

He was recruited to look after the tropical medicine programme and this he undertook with enormous enthusiasm. He was an administrator rather than a scientist but this did not stop him from encouraging people in the field. He travelled a great deal and was, I believe, of great help to the many people we were supporting overseas who needed concerned back-up from their home base.

After a few years, Tom developed an idea for putting over medical administration to medical officers working in country districts in the tropics. It was a play about a hypothetical country hospital and dispensary. Those using the teaching tool had to think about what they would do in various situations and how, for instance, they would obtain the necessary drugs and supplies to carry out their job. This exercise turned out to be very popular with WHO and students of tropical medicine. Having taken off in this direction, Tom decided to leave the Trust to take up a consultancy for the Commonwealth Secretariat which meant that he spent quite a lot of time overseas producing reports about the health state of various regions. He did this for a few years and then re-joined the Trust staff as director of the research unit in Nairobi, administering the programmes on schistosomiasis and hypertension. His administrative medical role with good links to the local medical community was important for these programmes and he was the originator of the scheme to set up research on the coast of Kenya and first identified Kilifi as the most suitable site.

CHAPTER 8

The History of Medicine

Again I revert to the will of Sir Henry Wellcome. This created two charities: the Museum and Library charity and the Medical Research charity. It could even be said that Wellcome would have put the former above the latter if he had been asked to choose between them. He had devoted most of the second half of his life to purchasing a magnificent collection of books and artefacts and I am sure, that when he died was much more interested in this field than medical research. Despite this bias, his will created a peculiar situation in that he left his collections and the monumental edifice "The Wellcome Building", which he had created to house them, in the care of the Wellcome Company and the charity in the charge of his trustees. Maybe even he did not perceive that the Company, although wholly owned by the Trustees, could neglect the history in favour of the pressing needs of the business or that charity law, or, at any rate, the Inland Revenue, would not permit the trustees to use tax-relieved funds to assist a library that belonged to a commercial organization.

The Company were not unduly neglectful and there were real accomodation problems because the Wellcome Building had become the headquarters of the business during the war. It was therefore largely occupied by the Company and the Wellcome Research Institution, and they sat in an uneasy balance between academic and commercial objectives. Over the years, the Company had stored the vast collections and even employed a limited number of staff to care for them but, they were able to make relatively little headway against such a mountain of material.

In 1960, when I joined the staff of the Trust there were two major figures in the Museum and Library, Dr E Ashworth Underwood and Dr Noel

Poynter. Underwood was the Director and Poynter was the Chief Librarian. Underwood was a dour unapproachable Scot who worked mostly at night and Poynter was a relatively young and ambitious man who found it very difficult to get on with Underwood. The result was two largely separate activities, a lively library and a dead museum, mostly packed away in storehouses in the suburbs.

I knew nothing about the subject of the history of medicine professionally but had always been disappointed at what little chance there had been as an undergraduate to get to know much about it, and particularly regretted that whenever anyone lectured about it, they always seemed to talk about the humours and black bile and other subjects which I found very dreary. I had bought Guthrie's book *A History of Medicine* but had fallen asleep on many occasions over its pages.

However in my post at the Trust the history of medicine was one of my concerns and I was asked by Lord Piercy to become Secretary of a History Committee set up to keep an eye on the activities of the newly acquired Museum and Library. Although the Trust had acquired the collections, the staff was still employed by the Foundation and the Committee was content with reports from the Foundation's representatives – Dr Adamson and Mr Falder – on their progress. The staff thus did not come under the offices of the Trust and so operated almost independently from their paymaster as well as their owners.

The problem of the future was muddied by the fact that Henry Dale was annoyed with Underwood because of his dilatoriness in producing his History of the Apothecaries and Boyd had formed a close relationship with Poynter in the Wellcome Building and sided with him against Underwood. Frank Green, the Trust's Scientific Secretary and my superior, was excluded from the History of Medicine because Piercy thought he was biased towards Poynter. All in all I had been given a baby which would need some nurturing.

I set about getting to know Poynter and Underwood individually both of whom were interesting characters. Underwood had a grudge against everyone who, over the years, had dispersed various parts of Wellcome's collection. He was a great believer in the importance of the collection but frustrated by the lack of funds to do anything with it. Poynter, on the other hand, was highly ambitious and had been able to get ahead with organising and cataloguing the Library and making it available to the public. He managed to persuade Boyd, not unreasonably, that things would progress better if he reported direct to the Trustees, and not through Underwood. Later in 1963 when Underwood retired, Poynter became the overall Director of the Museum and Library which was renamed The Institute in 1968.

Thus, by 1963, when the Trust was beginning to think more about its general policy, the history of medicine had become a significant part of its activities. Over the years, only two trustees had shown an interest (Boyd whose influence I have already mentioned and much later Paton). I thus found that an aspect of my responsibility merited no particular trustee knowledge or interest, but a feeling of obligation existed and hence a willingness to spend a reasonable percentage of the budget on it. The subject never came up for discussion unless I raised it but the trustees were pleased to see ideas which developed the concept and moved it forward. It was a challenging task but luckily I could turn to a growing number of enthusiasts for ideas and advice.

The central problem was that there was an enormous job to do creating the Library and Museum – which Poynter took on with talent and enthusiasm but there was so little interest in the wider world that one sometimes wondered if it was worth the effort.

However, Poynter was developing other aspects, especially in relation to organizations such as the Society of Apothecaries and The Osler Club, where medical men with an interest in history were to be found. The subject itself was still regarded as a fringe activity by serious historians. Unfortunately, Poynter did not wish anyone to challenge his position of self-assumed dominance in the field and he feared that university development would do just that. Everything for a while, therefore, centred on the Wellcome Institute, with its peculiar employment conditions and lack of direct responsibility to the administration of the Trust. This isolation prevented development of the type of broader thinking that would establish the subject's respectability in the academic world.

I worked away until by July 1967 the Trust was able to hold a three-day international symposium under the chairmanship of Lord Franks devoted to the Trust's role in the future of the history of medicine. This meeting and its recommendations, led to the Trust's establishing a History of Medicine Panel under the chairmanship of Lord Cohen of Birkenhead. The members came from the history of science, history, the Science Museum and there was a member from America and a Trustee, Lord Murray. I was its Secretary. It was not responsible for the Institute.

The Panel's earliest activity was to canvass the universities about their interest in the History of Medicine and to ask for proposals for the establishment of university academic Units. This meeting led to Units being created at Cambridge (1971), Oxford (1972), and a lectureship in Edinburgh, and, together with the sub-department at University College, London (to which Dr Edwin Clarke had now gone, following a period at the Wellcome Institute) initiated the Trust's involvement in its development as an academic subject. Dr Clarke's departure from the Wellcome Institute resulted from his proposal to Poynter that he should head up an academic department in the Institute. This Poynter much resented as it would have dented his position and his whole purpose to be academic leader of the history of medicine in England, in Europe and probably in the world – a position which he very largely achieved. While he had welcomed Clarke back from America, he did not foster his development or that of other historians. Poynter's achievements were considerable but not the academic development of the field which was his greatest wish. What he will always be remembered for was the creation of a fine library in excellent accommodation. In 1973, he retired to France and continued his writing but departed from the history of medicine scene in some degree of ill-health. He had performed an enormous service to the Institute but he had not created a successor, nor a succession for his own ideas. His great talent was tempered by his egocentricity.

Towards the end of Poynter's time, a proposal emanated from a discussion between me and Dr Frank Greenaway of the Science Museum, who was on our history advisory panel. I was concerned that the Museum exhibition was quite out of gear with the rest of our activities, historical and scientific. The collection did not generate academic history of medicine research and to exhibit it was expensive and the visitors were relatively few. If it moved to the Science Museum it would be properly catalogued and stored – a gargantuan task – and exhibited in a place where there were an enormous number of visitors. The trustees accepted the plan and I initiated discussions with the Science Museum, with a view to that institution taking over our museum's collections. It took several years to negotiate this transfer because of misunderstandings and legal quibbles but the agreement was eventually formalized in 1976 and the transfer began to take place.

This rationalisation set the seal on the Trust's new purpose in the context of the History of Medicine. The object now was to care for and develop Henry Wellcome's library and to encourage the development of the academic study of the subject to such a standard as to give it recognition as a field worthy of respect. When Edwin Clarke succeeded Noel Poynter he set about developing the Institute for this purpose and Eric Freeman took over the running of the library from Eric Gaskell.

Edwin Clarke was in post as director for six years and he remained a passionate student of the history of medicine. His most important publication was *The Human Brain and Spinal Cord* written with O'Malley. Neither a voluminous writer of articles, nor an avid lecturer, his objective was, simply, to recruit to the Institute an excellent academic group with the intention that they should have time to undertake scholarship in their fields of interest. His two most significant appointments were Roy Porter and Vivian Nutton from Cambridge. Porter and Nutton were doing very well in Cambridge but wanted to have fewer college duties to be able to get on with their research and writing. They arrived and, together with Christopher Lawrence, a medical graduate who had taken up medical history, they set about undertaking a busy research programme in the subject and, particularly for Porter, prolific writing and broadcasting activities. They also took on PhD students through the link with University College – where Bill Bynum had taken over. A joint committee with that institution permitted the creation of university standards for the staff of the Wellcome Institute –which also helped to create a salary structure related to the universities. Clarke had wished to develop other appointments in the Institute, particularly in the history of the biological sciences, but the Trustees began to be concerned about the over-growth of the centre compared with the academic units in the universities.

After giving him a free hand for the first five years, Edwin Clarke's reclusiveness began to worry me. Here was an institution that was extremely inward looking (except for Roy Porter) with no teaching programme at any level other than for PhD students. It really seemed much too secretive for the true development of the subject in relation to the outside world. I therefore asked Edwin whether he would consider developing an academic teaching programme. About a week after this interview, he came to me and said that he was the wrong man for doing that sort of job and so he thought that he would like to resign as director. He had made up his mind and it could not be changed so he retired. We then endeavoured to try and recruit a successor director and very nearly made an appointment of an English emigré to the US, but, in the end, his conditions were beyond our intended resources.

The Institute was, therefore, run for about a year by a committee under the chairmanship of Professor Rupert Hall which included Eric Freeman and Bill Bynum. Bill Bynum had by this time become integrated into the work of the Wellcome Institute despite still holding his university Senior Lectureship at UCL –indeed he was a candidate for the directorship.

However this direction by committee did not work very well I think because the resident members were rather too dominant and Rupert Hall not sufficiently stern. I therefore decided that I myself would like to manage the situation for a couple of years, and try and get some order into the unsatisfactory situation that had developed. The trustees agreed and when I took up the honorary directorship I got to know each member of the senior staff very well. What they really wanted was to develop a teaching programme and so I simply took the lid off the boiling pan. They were keen and ready to go and before long they developed a wide-ranging series of courses with an intercalated degree as well as other types of educational awards. After two years, the job was done and it was time I got back to my other expanding responsibilities.

We tried once more to appoint a director but failed. As related elsewhere, Sir William Paton had a considerable interest in the history of medicine and willingly took on the honorary directorship but unfortunately, after about a year, he fell ill and so although he remained as Honorary Director, the management of the Institute reverted to a joint committee of Bynum, Freeman and Emberton. In retrospect, it was not a good idea to have a trustee as the director as the other trustees accepted everything from the Institute on the nod and I found it very difficult to keep in touch without interfering. Later on, Eric Freeman was appointed as director in overall charge of the History of Medicine at the Trust and the Institute came under his general purview although it was accepted that the academic Unit would operate largely independently under Bynum. This was not a good solution but, since we could not identify an overall director of sufficient academic calibre, as well as administrative ability, to direct the whole place, it seemed the best arrangement at the time.

The many difficulties that have beset the Institute and the history of medicine generally over the years were a continuing problem for me. Nevertheless, I can look back on a quite remarkable transition from an uncatalogued library and museum in temporary shelving and largely in store, to the present state. It is a superbly accommodated library, a museum occupying special floors in the Science Museum, and an academic institution that is almost certainly the most respected in the world in the history of medicine. The subject had progressed from being a hobby of retired doctors to an academic subject in the same league as other aspects of history. The credit for this must go to the individuals who developed the library, the Science Museum activity, and the academic programme. All this without an overall leader of great ability after Poynter.

I must also record the considerable importance of having spread the subject more widely over the country through the Units in universities and the grants made through the History of Medicine Panel. All the eggs were not in one basket and a diversity of outlook could develop.

Finally as a personal addendum I should like to mention that in all my years associated with the History of Medicine I have had the advice and support of Professor Rupert Hall who in one position or another guided my steps. I had come to know Rupert because my wife Billie had taken an MSc degree in his department at Imperial College. I interviewed him in 1997 and his personal views are available in the transcript. He together with Ben Bembridge wrote *Physic and Philanthropy*. I also wish to acknowledge how Billie's research and activities in the history of various aspects of medicine guided me through troubled waters. Rupert and his wife Marie lived in a neighbouring village after they retired and I used to visit them each week until they both died in early 2009.

On 20 June 2008 one of the themes that I started came to fruition when Tilli Tansey was appointed Professor of The History of Modern Medical Sciences at University College, London. Readers will recall that when I was a medical student I wished to know more about the history of the subject but history always seemed to bear no relationship to the present day. This came home to me again when I worked in the Wellcome building. The Museum of Medical Science was completely separate from the historical activities. There were short accounts of the history of the discovery of tropical diseases in the Wellcome Museum of Medical Science but no one was apparently interested in studying the subject. Somehow historians of medicine could not encompass the modern scientific developments.

Tilli Tansey had come to see me as she wished to do a second PhD in the History of Medicine having obtained the first one in Physiology. I managed to arrange for her to be supported and she wrote her thesis on the early scientific career of Sir Henry Dale. His career had interested her because of her experience in Physiology. Here was the first attempt by a trained scientist with historical training to write about the history of modern medical science. I put the proposition to Rupert and Marie Hall who were preparing a report for me about the future of the history of medicine. They recommended that the Trust should encourage this aspect of history which would bridge the gap between our two main themes. Tilli was encouraged by David Gordon and Sir Christopher Booth, Harveian Librarian at the College of Physicians, who took a special interest in her activities. They cooperated in the holding of regular meetings called Wellcome Witnesses to Twentieth Century Medicine. I take at random Volume 23: *The Recent History of Platelets and Thrombosis and Other disorders*. The participants related their experiences and these were discussed by their contemporaries. The proceedings were recorded and then edited by Tilli and her colleagues. Tilli also wrote many books and papers. Included among these was a history of the Burroughs Wellcome Co. 1880-1940 co-authored with Roy Church.

A more personal aspect of this topic arose because Billie, my wife, had become interested in the history of tropical medicine when she had completed her thesis on the *Matter of Motion*. She was based in the Wellcome Museum of Medical Science and worked with others there to produce films about the history of sleeping sickness. Subsequently when we retired we started a project to get multiple authors to write *An Illustrated History of Tropical Diseases*. It was taken to completion and published by the Wellcome Trust under the editorship of Frank Cox.

CHAPTER 9

The Wellcome Research Laboratories in England and their collaboration with the USA

I have decided to recount the story of the Wellcome Laboratories at Beckenham in Kent as a separate chapter. My reason for doing this is because Sir Henry had kept them as part of his domain along with the History of Medicine when he transferred the main responsibility for the business to George Pearson. As a consequence of this separation and the nature of their organisation the laboratories saw themselves as an independent research institution. As such they had a remarkable record of achievement and many of their staff went on to hold important positions in academic institutions and became Fellows of the Royal Society. The directors of the laboratories saw this as their freedom to do their own science and so were resistant to attempts to make them more orientated to the function of industrial research laboratories aimed at discovering new products for the Company to sell.

Unfortunately after Wellcome's death in 1936 there were insufficient funds for such an independent role alongside the need for a dedicated industrial laboratory. The staff on tenured appointments continued with their individual projects and many of these enterprises had run out of steam. Perrin, the Chairman of the Company tried to make changes and some profitable products were discovered but it took many years to adjust to this different role.

From the point of view of this book I have decided to draw on the information published as *In Pursuit of Excellence* by the Company in 1980 in

71

the centenary year of its foundation. It tells a fascinating story of many great achievements especially in the role of the prophylaxis and treatment of diphtheria, German measles and tetanus.

Wellcome Research

Research and the scientific developments in the treatment of disease were always close to the heart of Henry Wellcome and provided him with constant intellectual challenges. The diphtheria bacillus had been discovered in 1883 and the endotoxin it produces was described in 1888. Two years later, in 1890 it was established that the injection of small, sub-lethal doses of the toxin into animals would induce the production of an antitoxin. When this antiserum was collected and then injected into other animals it provided protection against a lethal dose level of the diphtheria toxin. The use of this technique to induce antitoxin production in a sheep was successfully used to treat a girl with diphtheria in Germany. This was a major breakthrough as diphtheria was the commonest cause of childhood mortality in Europe and North America. There were 8000 childhood deaths per year during the decade of the 1890s in England and Wales.

Wellcome realised the need to be able to manufacture large quantities of a standardised, high quality diphtheria antiserum on a commercial basis. In 1894 the Wellcome Physiological Research Laboratories were established in modest premises in Charlotte Street in central London. As horses were the main power sources for everyday transport needs, eight horses in a nearby stable were available to generate the antiserum. The first batch of equine antiserum was released for therapy in 1885.

Demand for Wellcome diphtheria antiserum soon outstripped supply, particularly when a standardised method of production had been reported by Ehrlich in Germany in 1887. Large quantities were required not only for local use but also there was a considerable demand from New York where diphtheria was rampant. In 1898 Wellcome transferred the Physiological Research Laboratories to a 10 acre site at Brocken Hall, Herne Hill in South-east London. Dr Walter Dowson was appointed director in 1890 and he was succeeded by Henry Dale in 1906.

John Mellanby who later became a Fellow of the Royal Society was the first research biologist appointed at the Laboratories. Mellanby spent several years studying equine globulins and other serum proteins and he described a method for concentrating diphtheria antitoxin without denaturation of the protein. He achieved this by treating the serum with alcohol at low temperatures and this method was further developed by Cohn. In 1904, at the age of 22, A T Glenny was the first person to detoxify diphtheria toxin with formalin and use this formalinised toxin to immunise horses for the production of antitoxin. As the First World War raged there was a great demand for large quantities of diphtheria and tetanus antitoxins, anti-gas gangrene sera and typhoid vaccines for the armed forces. From his youthful start at the laboratories Glenny went on to manage the production of antisera for Wellcome for another forty years.

During the early part of the century many research opportunities were tackled by the laboratories. In 1922 the laboratories were moved again, this time to a 108 acre site at Langley Court, Beckenham, Kent. Glenny and his team made significant advances in the production and standardisation of medical and veterinary antisera and vaccines. Glenny and Südmersen were the first to enunciate the principles of primary and secondary stimulus in immunisation in 1921. In 1923, Glenny, Allen and Hopkin were the first to suggest that diphtheria toxoid be used for the active immunisation of healthy children as a preferable alternative to the use of heterologous antiserum for treatment after they had developed diphtheria. Glenny and his colleagues discovered the adjuvant effect of alum on diphtheria toxoid in 1926, and advocated the human use of toxoid antitoxin floccules (TAF) in 1927. They then developed the highly antigenic alum precipitated toxoid (APT) which became the standard preparation for diphtheria immunisation. Glenny was elected a Fellow of the Royal Society. Some of his other honours included the prestigious Jenner Medal in 1952 and the Addingham Medal in 1955, the latter bearing the inscription:

"To the individual who has made the most valuable discovery for relieving pain and suffering in humanity."

Tetanus was a major cause of death and the collaboration between Glenny and O'Brien at Wellcome and Brigadier Boyd of the War Office resulted in the immunization of the army against tetanus just before the outbreak of war in 1939. During the Second World War Wellcome produced thirty million doses of tetanus toxoid as well as large quantities of life-saving tetanus and gas-gangrene antitoxins.

Work at the laboratories was extended to include the study of viruses. A yellow fever vaccine was produced at the Wellcome laboratories in Beckenham during the Second World War. The Laboratories were the first to produce and be licensed to distribute the Sabin type live attenuated polio virus vaccine rather than the killed Salk type. Other vaccines followed such as "Alemevax" which was developed from an attenuated rubella virus strain. The important point of this development was that the vaccine was prepared using human cells rather than animal derived tissue which eliminated the potential dangers of exposure to animal derived pathogens.

Many other important discoveries were made by the research biochemists, bacteriologists, virologists and immunologists at Beckenham. The work on bacterial vaccines led to the discovery of the importance of antigenic competition. This knowledge led to the balancing of the diptheria, pertussis and tetanus antigens into a triple vaccine for administration to infants, namely "Trivax". The production of standard diagnostic preparations at Beckenham had been pioneered by Harry Proom and they were in demand by other laboratories. Initially these had been supplied free of charge but a commercial company, Wellcome Reagents Limited was then established with headquarters at Hither Green in London, supplying more than 400 products. Success of this part of the business was due to the development of the haemagglutination and latex haemagglutination test for pregnancy and to detect thyroid antibody, coagulation disorders and hepatitis antigen.

Research from 1944 to 1980

In 1944 Dr C.H. Kellaway joined the company as Research Director in chief. He succeeded Dr Wenyon. Dr Kellaway made a major contribution to the way that research was conducted in the Company. He not only understood that more resources for chemical and pharmacological research had to be found if Wellcome was to discover new medicines on the scale of other companies but he realised that the research units and even the departments within them tended to act independently of each other. This had to change. Research work was taking place at Beckenham, Esher and Dartford. In 1946 a new building was erected at Beckenham to accommodate a much enlarged organic chemistry unit as well as an enlarged antibacterial chemotherapy section. In addition this move allowed for the much needed expansion of pharmacological research. New and exciting products were soon to come out of this building.

The Wellcome Company had been involved in the early commercial development of penicillin but this was not a success. However, the work of the antibiotic research unit continued and resulted in the discovery of polymyxin. This was the second successful antibiotic to be discovered in the UK and was eventually formulated into a very successful topical antibiotic that was effective against many bacteria resistant to penicillin. This development was a prime example of collaborative team work and involved research teams with expertise in chemistry, chemotherapy, mycology and industrial fermentation.

The re-organisation and collaborative working policies instituted by Dr Kellaway were rewarded by the success of the chemical team led by Dr D W Adamson who worked closely with a pharmacological group led by Dr A F Green. During the period 1946 to 1951 they discovered no fewer than five novel compounds that became marketed products. The first of these discoveries was procyclidine "Kemadrin" which was used for many years to control the debilitating symptoms of Parkinson's disease and to control drug-induced extrapypyramidal syndromes. Another important drug was diethlythiambutene "Themalon" which was a powerful analgesic and hypnotic that was particularly suitable for canine surgery, especially as its actions could be readily terminated by nalorphine, which, as "Lethidrone", had recently been made available by the Company. Nevertheless, the most important compound discovered was triprolidine which, under the name of "Actidil" or with L(+) pseudoephedrine as "Actifed", gave Wellcome a world-class antihistamine and a nasal decongestant

The process of research integration continued and the Therapeutic Research Division was created under RSF Hennessey. This Division incorporated the Chemical and Pharmacological Laboratories in Beckenham and the Wellcome Laboratories of Tropical Medicine in London, which moved to the site at Beckenham in 1965. Not all of the Beckenham site was focused on primary research. Much of the activity had now to be turned to provide the essential toxicology and pharmacokinetic studies needed to develop the new therapeutic agents.

Undoubtedly one of the most exciting scientific, medical and commercial success stories in the history of the Company is that of allopurinol. Discovery of allopurinaol resulted from the search for inhibitors of xanthine oxidase which might enhance the therapeutic effects of 6-mercaptopurine. These inhibitors proved to have the important effect of preventing the formation of uric acid. "Zyloric" or "Zyloprim" was the first compound found to have this property and became the drug of choice for the treatment of gout and other conditions associated with urate disorder.

Treatment with 6-mercaptopurine had been found to depress antibody production and to prolong the survival of kidney grafts in animals. Azathioprine "Imuran" was synthesised by the team searching for a drug that released 6-mercaptopurine slowly after administration. However, azathioprine was found to be superior to 6-mercaptopurine and less toxic. It became the first compound to be accepted as effective in preventing graft rejection in humans and became an essential part of the transplant treatment protocol. During the six years taken by the Food and Drugs Administration in the USA to satisfy themselves of the safety and acceptable risk:benefit ratio of "Imuran" the Burroughs Wellcome Co. supplied the drug free of charge to almost every recipient of a kidney transplant in the United States.

Research collaboration between the United Kingdom and United States led to the discovery and development of co-trimoxazole "Septrin". During the 1950s research by Dr SRM Bushby and his colleagues at Beckenham had identified the antibacterial potential of trimethoprim. In the USA Dr. Hitchings and his colleagues showed that this effect was due to the antimetabolite properties of triomethoprim at a particular stage of metabolism within the bacteria. They also confirmed that the effects of sulphonomides occurred at another metabolic point and went on to postulate that a combination of trimethoprim and sulphonamide would have a powerful synergistic action. Laboratory studies and subsequent clinical trials confirmed this hypothesis. "Septrin", a combination of trimethoprim and sulphonamide, became a major antibiotic with a world-wide market for the treatment of urinary tract and respiratory infections, and gonococcal urethritis as well as typhoid and paratyphoid fevers. Together with Zyloric it played a major role in transforming the Group into one of the largest British pharmaceutical companies.

In 1973 an outstanding pharmacologist, JR Vane, joined the Company as the Group Research and Development Director. He played an active part in initiating or encouraging work in several new fields including his own particular area of expertise the prostaglandins. A notable success was the discovery of prostacyclin, the most potent of known inhibitors of platelet aggregation, which has an important physiological role in the prevention of thrombus formation. In 1982 Sir John Vane, FRS, was a joint winner of the Nobel Prize for Medicine for his work on prostaglandins.

CHAPTER 10

The Chairmanship of Sir David Steel

When Sir David Steel took over the Chairmanship of the Trust there was a vast change. Instead of isolating the Company from the Trust he sought to involve his fellow trustees in the management of their whole responsibility. No longer was the Company a remote body with only one channel of communication from chairman to chairman. He went to see Alfred Shepperd and asked him why the dividend to the trustees was so low and Shepperd said it was very reasonable for a private Company. What Shepperd might have mentioned was that since Michael Perrin's time the trustees had agreed that 70% of the profits should be retained for development of the Company but he did not and Steel also did not know about this decision. Shepperd's response irritated Steel and almost certainly led on to him wanting to dig deeper.

Steel had simply pursued the course that had always been his way in the management of BP. When he joined the Trust Shepperd thought Steel would be vulnerable to his high handed style. He had not been able to use this style with Franks because he would never have given room for such an approach. In fact, nor was Steel but he did not convey the same headmaster-like aura that Franks did. However what Shepperd did not realise was that when anyone showed Steel such an attitude his hackles rose and he began to suspect that there was a problem. If Shepperd had considered Steel's war record where he had been awarded a DSO and MC and was three times mentioned in dispatches he might have realised what would happen. He could not have risen to the chairmanship of BP if he was vulnerable to such tactics.

David said that he wished to get to know more about the activities of the

77

Company and for the scientific trustees to become familiar with the research programmes. As a consequence David and I started a round of visits to the Company's installations at Dartford, the factory, Crewe the headquarters of Calmic and Berkhamstead the headquarters of Cooper, McDougall and Robertson. All the trustees visited North Carolina once a year to hear about the United States business and their research progress. We all went to Beckenham once a year and I took David to visit the Trust's activities overseas. We went to the Company branches in India, Singapore, Thailand, Australia and New Zealand, Brazil etc. During the overseas visits, we obtained a considerable insight into the Company's affairs. We were not probing but just becoming informed of our responsibilities.

David also sought the advice of Flemings the merchant bankers on the finances of the Company. A study was undertaken by Lawrence Banks and he reported to the trustees. His views are described in the account of the sales in the next chapter.

In the meanwhile David had asked the trustees to appoint Roger Gibbs as a new trustee to give him support in the negotiations that would arise in the City if any sale of shares was to be contemplated. Visits had to be made to the Charity Commission to get permission and the stipulations in the Will required legal advice. All this had to be undertaken without the knowledge of Shepperd who was against any change, having enjoyed the situation with Franks by which he did not have any contact with the trustees. I think he could not believe that the decision to sell shares had been made without his knowledge

When Shepperd died in 2008 his obituary in the *Daily Telegraph* said that he had persuaded the trustees to sell shares. This was completely untrue. He was very much against such a move.

Once the trustees had visited the Company's installations they could form their own view and when Lawrence Banks had reported on his analysis it became apparent that the Trust simply had to consider offloading some of its shareholding because it was so out of balance and in danger of a disaster such as Nuffield had experienced when the car company failed. The sale of shares which became imperative would of course lead to an improved income for the Trust and remove the need to try and get a larger share of the Company's profits.

Once the shares had been sold the trustee's position was completely changed. The visits to the company branches had to stop and so its progress could only be managed as if it was any other investment.

Naturally it therefore became less interesting than when we were meeting the people in the research laboratories, the management and the factories. It was a very sad day when eventually the Company was sold to Glaxo and all the activities were absorbed and many loyal staff of the Company lost their jobs. Science in Commerce is very different from science in academia! The charitable Trust had become very rich but Wellcome's initial creation, the pharmaceutical company, had disappeared taking all its history and employees with it. I do not think that was the objective of Henry Wellcome but an inevitable result of the success of his creation in the world of today.

Sir David Steel

David Steel was identified as the successor Chairman to Lord Franks, at the suggestion of the Bank of England. He was in his last year as Chairman of BP and extremely busy. He therefore did not take up his trusteeship until about six months before Franks departed and they had virtually no overlap. David Steel was a solicitor by training who had spent most of his working life with BP, with a spell in the United States. He was therefore essentially "the man of business" type of trustee envisaged in Henry Wellcome's will. But he was not a businessman in the sense of being a salesman. Essentially he was a charming leader of the Board of BP with its enormous political and Government overtones. David Steel's role at the Trust was to carry forward its policies and to develop the interrelationship with the Company. He therefore developed, as had not been done before, a business-like relationship with the Company.

David led the decision to take the Company public. He was at the helm when the enormous and detailed responsibility for the first sale of shares took place. He took this responsibility in a quite remarkably relaxed but determined way.

He and Lady Anne Steel were a great asset during this developmental time. He took an interest in everything that was shown to him and made it possible to advance the scientific work of the Trust. He listened to proposals and analysed the wider implications of their support. David Steel was easy to get on with, a good companion on our travels and great fun at a number of days on the golf course with Gordon Smith and Roger Gibbs. If only Franks had played golf! Anne was a great companion when Billie and I travelled with them.

> The Wellcome Trust and medical research as a whole owe David Steel a great debt of gratitude.

The next chapter is an account of the sale of Wellcome shares and the final transfer to Glaxo, written for this book by Neil Collins, as its intricacies were quite outside my experience.

CHAPTER 11

Selling the Wellcome Trust's Stake in the Company

The financial and investment story of the Wellcome Trust is, in its own way, as remarkable as the medical and scientific one. By the time the death duties had been paid on Sir Henry Wellcome's will, the assets under the Trust's control amounted to £1.1 million. Today, the Trust's assets are close to £15 billion, and that is after giving away a similar amount in grants for research. This is the story of three key events in that financial transformation.

The chairman of BP could be as tough as his name implied. Sir David Steel had reached the top of the oil giant in 1975, and had won a war of attrition against Tony Benn, who, as energy minister, had wanted to nationalise North Sea oil. The experience taught him a great deal about the relationship between a majority shareholder and a company's board, because the Government then owned 68% of BP following the Bank of England's crude rescue of Burmah Oil at Christmas 1974.

It was to stand him in good stead sooner than he thought. At BP, he was used to robust argument around the boardroom table, so his arrival at the Wellcome Trust in 1982 caused him something of a surprise. As he recalled in 1996: "The trustees were on their best behaviour. I found that there wasn't the sort of discussion I'd been used to at BP."

When Franks first took the chair, he had insisted that he was the only contact with the Company. All communication was to be between him and the chairmen of the day – Sir Michael Perrin, Andy Gray and Sir Alfred Shepperd alone. In the early years, this curious arrangement had worked quite well, especially since the Trustees were nearly all eminent scientists with little understanding of finance. Yet Franks was growing old, and his chosen successor, Lord Armstrong, had died suddenly.

Steel, then in his last year at BP, was a logical choice for such an important but hardly full-time role, and after that first board meeting in 1982, Franks stepped down to make way for him. The glaringly obvious question could now be addressed: was the Trust in charge of the Company, or was it the other way round?

Between the years 1950 and 1979 nearly 70% of the net profit of the Company after tax was ploughed back and not distributed to its 100% shareholder. Without this the Company would not have been able to grow at the pace it did. Franks could not see any reason to change this during his chairmanship. When interviewed in 1991, nine years after he retired, he said

"I thought there would be a time when the business so expanded that it would be impossible to maintain the existing relationship between the Trust and the Company – the question was when was that time – I did not think it had arrived in my time because I calculated that the Trust was doing better out of the Company than it would have done out of a normal portfolio. It was more profitable and was growing very fast and growing in profitability. The other potential danger was of all the Trust's eggs being in one basket, mainly the Wellcome Foundation, and I remembered the Nuffield Foundation and its fate."

Steel not only saw the Nuffield warning, but could see the lack of financial heavyweights among the scientists of the Trust board. He had got to know Roger Gibbs while the two of them were saving the Mermaid Theatre in the City. Gibbs was both highly respected and hugely popular in the City's money markets. He had 35 years in the City culminating in becoming chairman of Gerrard & National, the biggest of the discount houses, which provided the lubrication between the Bank of England and the other users of the money markets.

Crucially, Gibbs also had first-hand experience of the Nuffield tragedy. His father, Sir Geoffrey Gibbs, had been chairman of the Foundation from 1951 to 1973, and spent many Sunday afternoons visiting Lord Nuffield at Huntercombe, his home nearly 20 miles outside Oxford, trying to persuade the great man to allow diversification. Every time, he returned home frustrated. At one stage Nuffield had wanted to give him the Huntercombe golf course, but the cautious Gibbs was suspicious. Is it on common land? he enquired of the generous Lord. Well, yes, came the reply. Does it make a loss? Er, yes, but only a small one. The offer was declined.

In 1948 the Nuffield Foundation, built on Nuffield's Morris Motors, a business that had prospered during the war and then, at its zenith, was 40 times the size of the Wellcome Trust. Nuffield was adamant: "My Foundation rises or falls on the fortunes of my original bicycle shop," he was quoted as saying. As the British motor industry crumbled, it fell, never to rise again. It now disburses around £9 million a year, or less than 2% of the annual grants made by the Wellcome Trust.

As the new boy, Steel was understandably cautious, but if the first board meeting had been a surprise, his first meeting with Shepperd was a shock. In his career at BP Steel had understood the importance of giving everyone, including his subordinates, a fair say before a decision was reached. A man of considerable charm, he explained that he did not think the Trust was getting its fair share of the profits in annual dividends. Shepperd retorted: "For a private company, you're doing pretty well." This was not an auspicious start.

Steel said later: "Shep was unused to being interfered with by what we were, the owners of the Company." On his return, he told the other trustees "This fellow is impossible to deal with." The second meeting, after Gibbs had joined in February 1983, was no better. Says Gibbs: "Steel had remarked that Shep had not seemed very pleased to see us. I could hardly believe my ears when Shep said, albeit with the hint of a smile: "The problem is that I don't like people, except, of course, my young grandson in America'." Essentially, Shepperd made it plain to them that the Company was none of their business. Before the arrival of Steel the trustees never discussed the finances of the Company. They were not allowed to visit, and simply accepted what Shep said they could have.

This was hardly a basis for harmony, but Steel denied later that he had picked Gibbs because he'd already decided the *status quo* could not continue. "I needed a bit of support because the trustees were highly intelligent but they weren't involved in the ways of the City." There were two worlds, science and money, and they hardly talked the same language. The Trust's portfolio was simple, if absurdly lop-sided: it owned 100% of the shares in a company which was clearly worth hundreds of millions of pounds, alongside a portfolio of £35 million, mainly the reserve to pay grants already awarded and mostly deposited with Local Authorities. There was no Finance or Investment Committee.

The unbalanced portfolio made the Trustees' task of supporting medical science difficult. On the one hand, the success of the business was generating a substantial income flow from dividends, while, on the other, it emphasised the dependence on a single asset. Henry Wellcome's will, drawn up in 1932, had envisaged the Company – confusingly then called the Foundation – remaining as a permanent asset of the Trust. It did not specifically exclude the possibility of a sale, but it demanded "exceptional circumstances" to justify such a step.

Yet the risks to the Trust's long-term health were already plain enough: the pharmaceutical industry, always susceptible to Government interference, might be subjected to unilateral price cuts, or even nationalised. The Company might make some hideous mistake, and the now forgotten dreadful tragedy of Thalidomide was still in people's minds.

The choice before the trustees was between soldiering on while increasing the pressure on the Company to pay out higher dividends, an outright sale of the Company, or a Stock Exchange flotation. The sale would have been easy enough to arrange, but it was unlikely to maximise the value of a business which, however high-minded and concerned with improving the lot of mankind through medical research, had been run more for the benefit of the Company than the shareholder.

A flotation was hardly straightforward, either. The 1932 Will, now 54 years old, had made no clear distinction between the Company and the Trust, but the conflict between the will and the trustees' fiduciary duty was growing. Steel approached the Charity Commissioners for a resolution. Rather to his surprise, he met with a sympathetic response from the chairman, Denis Peach, who pointed to some 1967 legislation designed to deal with such problems, and which gave Steel much more flexibility than he had expected. Indeed, Peach said that the trustees' fiduciary duty obliged them to think actively about diversification.

Gibbs's first trustee meeting, on 1 February 1983, gave him some idea of what was to come. That meeting was followed by the Company's AGM, consisting of twelve Wellcome directors, seven trustees and Peter Williams, sitting round the boardroom table. All but one of the company directors was an executive, effectively dependent on Shepperd. It was not a forum to encourage robust debate.

A week later Steel and Gibbs had a quiet drink together, and discussed the possibility of taking the Company public. They compiled a list of a dozen merchant banks which they could approach to handle a flotation, eventually whittling it down to three. Two of them, Barings and Warburg, were working for the Company, so they went to see Robert Fleming and met and got to know Lawrence Banks. As Gibbs put it later: "The poor trustees, who had been used to thinking about science and medicine, had to understand about 'concert parties', 'green shoes' and other extraordinary technical financial expressions."

The new trustees also started to look more closely at their main asset. Gibbs recalls a visit to Burroughs Wellcome in America, and the gleaming contrast with the rather pedestrian business in Britain. Nobel prizes had been won by Henry Dale, after he left the Company and before they joined Wellcome by John Vane and James Black. The US company, had developed the world-changing compounds which produced two Nobel Prize winners, George Hitchings and Gertrude Elion.

When the Americans showed the trustees the confidential 10-year projections for sales, they could scarcely believe their eyes. They agreed not to discuss them with the Wellcome board on their return. Just how glittering the prospects were was confirmed when the visitors received an informal approach from the Burroughs Wellcome management to buy them out for $1 billion.

Continuing as before, even if the dividend were to be raised substantially, was clearly no longer a realistic option. As Banks put it later: "You had a set of trustees invested in a company which on the face of it was not being all that brilliantly managed, in an industry which was highly competitive and which had obvious vulnerabilities. It was dependent on a relatively small number of products with a reasonable but not indefinite patent life. It was spending a huge amount on R&D which in Britain did not look very productive. I'm far from clear even now that the investment has been recovered by the Company, let alone a multiple of it." The cost of compliance needed to develop and bring a drug to market was rising strongly. Yet, as it turned out, Banks's observation was more accurate than he could have known. By the first quarter of 1985, the decision to float had effectively been taken. The Company was completely in the dark, and when Shepperd was told, confidentially, what was to happen, he was shocked, but he agreed to keep the plan secret. Only when he – quite reasonably – insisted on telling his board, did it instantly leak, in the *Sunday Telegraph*. Ironically, one of the *Telegraph*'s New Year predictions for January was of a Wellcome flotation. It had been a guess.

The case may have been clear to the trustees, but the Company had different interests. Steel recalled: "I remember going to board meetings when

85

they looked very po-faced. They wondered if they would see their whole position changed and were highly suspicious. The only thing that helped was when we told them: 'You have a chance of getting some share options.' That changed attitudes. But I don't blame them. They had a very good life and careers. They were running what they thought was a Wellcome closed shop, so to speak, and they were naturally suspicious of any change."

Preparing the way for what was likely to be the biggest flotation of a private company the London market had ever seen was a laborious process. Banks's first guess at the value had been around £500 million, but it quickly became clear that this figure was much too low. Wellcome would get into the FTSE 100 share index, whose constituents are determined by the market value of London-listed companies, with a full weighting provided the "free float" exceeded 25% of the shares in issue. Getting into the index would oblige many large funds to buy the shares at almost any price, whereas a lesser sale would allow them to be much more choosey. Again with one eye on their fiduciary duty, the trustees saw that 25% was the minimum they could sell.

Thus started what one participant called "the first contested flotation in the stock market's history". Shepperd resisted strongly. Gibbs said later: "He could have delayed us wishing to go public if he had only gone some way towards what David Steel was asking, a much greater dividend. He really did make a mistake from that point of view." However, once the process started, it gained its own momentum, and it became clear that no realistic increase in the Wellcome dividend would solve the other problems about the Trust's portfolio.

The long drawn-out drama of the flotation process, with every participant sweating over every word in a document few would read, and even fewer fully comprehend, came to a head with the final pricing meeting at Flemings in February 1986. Shepperd dug in his heels and demanded a sale price of 110p a share, a level which the trustees and Banks considered ridiculously low. As Gibbs put it: "If you want to be nasty and cynical you could say they were all going to get options. It would be libellous to suggest that that was the only motive for management, but it must have been in the backs of their minds...They wanted to see a 'successful' float, with a nice big premium.

To be fair, the directors did not want to set the thing off on a basis which was valuing a lot of hope factor, and which could subsequently have rebounded back to their discredit and, to a certain extent, the headline –

'Charitable Trust fobs off public with overpriced stock' or some such.

So concerned was Banks at this possibility that he asked David Brewerton, a former City Editor of *The Times,* to write the leader the paper might have published had the sale flopped. He used this to make the point to the trustees of the reputational risk of over-pricing the issue. The leader concluded gravely: "Wellcome plc might just pause a moment to reflect that the commercial behaviour which eventually drove its sponsor to sell out might, one day, be called into question by its customers." Since the Company was not encouraging the sale, this was hardly fair, but it served to make the point about the risk to its reputation.

While 110p a share was patently too cheap, the pricing meeting lasted three hours, and Shepperd hauled his advisers from the room twice. According to Gibbs: "It was a particularly testing afternoon. We eventually said, 'It's 120p and that's that'." One attraction of this price was that it valued Wellcome at just over the £1 billion mark, or almost on a par with Glaxo, the UK's biggest and most highly-rated pharmaceutical company.

The Trust raised £200 million, and the Company £50 million ("quite why, I'm unclear," Banks recalled). It looked like nothing more than a comfort blanket to face the harsh spotlight of public ownership, since Wellcome plc already had net cash on its balance sheet. In fact, Shepperd was sticking to his sensible maxim, that one should raise money when the opportunity arises, rather than when it was needed.

The issue price was never seen again. The public, both institutions and private buyers, could spot a bargain when it was set in front of them, and the offer was five times subscribed. Applications were heavily scaled down, and at the close of the first day's hectic trading, the price was 175p. Prominent among the buyers were the investment managers at Mercury Asset Management, part of SG Warburg, whose corporate financiers had advised the Company's directors to hold out for 110p.

At a stroke, the finances of the Trust were transformed. It had a cash sum nearly ten times the size of its accumulated reserves, and the prospect of bigger annual dividends on its 75% holding in the Company than it had previously had on its 100%, thanks to the pressure to distribute more generously to the new shareholders. The shares proved a fine investment for the new holders, too, helped by a single, guarded sentence in that voluminous prospectus.

Wellcome's drug portfolio included AZT. Marketed as Retrovir, it seemed like the world's only defence against a new Black Death, the

scourge of AIDS. In February 1985, the Royal College of Nursing demon-
strated that it was better at patient care than it was at maths by extrapo-
lating the data and predicting that the number of AIDS cases in Britain
would reach a million by 1991. In fact by the end of that year, confirmed
cases had reached just 275, but the nurses had helped send the Government
into full panic mode, and £2.5 million was spent on a bizarre public health
campaign telling people not to die from ignorance.

The timing of the scare could hardly have been better for Wellcome. As
the panic spread, although the disease didn't (by 2005, the total number of
cases in Britain had reached 20,099, with 13,386 deaths) investors piled
into the shares. No respectable portfolio could be seen without them, and
by the end of 1989 the price had soared to 860p. The problem that the
trustees had sought to ameliorate with the sale was only too obvious once
again. The goose was laying golden eggs all right, but it was still only one
goose. The trustees considered a second share sale, but the shares fell back
to under 500p and the pressure eased.

However, the AIDS obsession continued. Banks recalled one particular
episode: "There had been at least a couple of occasions between 1988 and
1991 when we were tossing up whether it was time to sell. At the end of
1991 there was some lunatic at University College London who said that
Retrovir taken with other drugs would cure AIDS. The stock rose from
970p to almost £12. It was a scandalous piece of misinformation."

Nevertheless, it concentrated the minds of the trustees. They realised
they had to deal with the new circumstances. To outsiders, the difficulties
of a further sale might seem less than those of the initial public offering.
After all, the shares are already priced by the market, there's a track record
for the Company in the public eye, and analysts are familiar with the business. Yet in many ways, the second offering was going to be much harder to pull off successfully.

For a start, Wellcome was a much more valuable property than it had
been before the flotation. It was big enough to warrant an international
spread of shareholders, but few financial institutions outside Britain knew
anything about it. Simply trickling the shares onto the market to meet pass-
ing demand was never an option, because each sale would have to be
declared, the potential buyers would realise that there were plenty more to
come, and the price would quickly start to suffer. Besides, the big US institutions would not be interested in acquiring what to them represented
penny packets of shares. If they were to buy, they wanted a significant

investment.

In 1989 Steel had retired, and Gibbs became chairman. Shepperd retired in June 1990, and the trustees seized the opportunity to split the roles. Sir Alistair Frame, the well-respected former chairman of Rio Tinto, took the chair. He was a popular choice "utterly delightful and very shareholder conscious" said Gibbs. John Robb, who had been recruited as Shepperd's deputy, became chief executive. When Shepperd retired, the dividend was a well-covered 5.05p, and Gibbs pressed Frame for a big rise. He recalled later: "When the results were announced in early November, we were expecting something in the region of 7½ to 8p a share and we got only 6 ½p. So I was immediately on the telephone to Alistair to say how bitterly disappointed we were. He replied: 'My problem is very simple. Some of the non-executives have been here for six or seven years. I've been here for a few months. Give me one more year. And of course we gave him one more year and twelve months later the dividend was put up, not to the 8p we were expecting, but to 10p."

When Gibbs and Sir Peter Cazalet, newly elected as a trustee, went to see Frame and Robb, they said how pleased they were, but warned them that they were looking very carefully at their shareholding. "Alistair saw it coming a mile off," says Gibbs. "John Robb was somewhat stunned." The Wellcome will had specified that there had to be an "unavoidable reason" for the trustees to sell the Company, and when Robb arrived he was comforted in the knowledge of having a 75% shareholder which appeared to be permanent. Now, it seemed, the shareholder was prepared to cede control.

The logic was driving events again. In early 1992 Gibbs applied to the High Court, before Mr Justice (later Lord) Hoffmann for permission to cut the Trust's holding to below 50%. Hoffmann, then 58, confessed that he'd been out the evening before, that he hadn't read the papers, and could Gibbs and his team return in the afternoon? "Well," says Gibbs, "we had no choice but to agree, so we returned at 2.30. He'd not only read the papers, but got the whole thing to a tee."

The Company, which argued that the Trust had a duty to maintain a majority stake in it permanently, was comprehensively Hoffmanned. Gibbs recalls: "He said he'd done a few sums, and calculated that if the Trust grew its assets in the next 10 years at the same rate as it had in the last 10, we'd own the whole world. He added: 'You seem to know what you're doing. Go below 50%, or under 25% if you like."

Armed with the legal ruling, the trustees announced their intention to sell more, and decided to set the size of the sale by first assessing the demand. The numbers were far too big for a purely domestic sale – the privatisation of BT, for example, had raised a then-record £3.2 billion – so the Company and its advisers hit the road to sell the stock to the big American institutions.

Thus began a gruelling five months, trying to sell to the world's financial institutions the idea of becoming shareholders in Wellcome. These were, and are, concentrated in the US, but one tour took the road show through four European centres, Amsterdam, Paris, Madrid and Frankfurt, in a single day. "It just went on and on," recalled Gibbs.

It was not only exhausting, but very expensive. The US banks have a stranglehold on such major sales of shares. The total effective cost amounted to 6.65% of the proceeds, far more than London banks would expect to charge, and there were understandable rumblings from the Charity Commissioners. Yet the issue was too big to be purely domestic, and there were advantages in getting the Wellcome name better known in the world's biggest market for pharmaceuticals.

The initial maximum number of shares to be sold was 417 million, which would have taken the Trust's holding down to 25%, but it quickly became clear that this was too much, even for an international issue. By the time the prospectus was published, the maximum had been cut to 330 million, and in the event, to avoid too big a discount to the prevailing market price, the final sale was of 270 million, yielding £144 million in fees to the army of advisers, and taking the Trust's stake in Wellcome down to just under 40%.

There were other difficulties, too. John Robb was understandably nervous at the prospect of the comfort blanket of a 75%, relatively passive shareholder selling down below a majority stake. He had only recently stepped up to chief executive, and knew that ICI, then a powerhouse of the British economy with a rapidly-growing drugs business, was often talked about as a possible buyer of Wellcome.

He extracted a "memorandum of understanding" from the trustees that they would not agree to a sale of further shares without first consulting the Company board. This was to cause much bad blood later. In actual fact, says Banks, it was a case of the dog that didn't bark. One would have thought that the sale of such a strategic stake presented an unmissable opportunity to all potential predators. But "nobody showed up with a cheque book".

Then there was the question of timing. A General Election could not be delayed beyond June 1992, and there was the inevitable speculation about when John Major would call it. He did so in mid-March, for April 9. Although Hoffmann had ruled that the Court would accept the trustees' proposal, it still had to be fitted into the High Court's schedule to be rubber-stamped. It was not until the first of May that the Court and the Charity Commissioners formally ruled that the sale could proceed.

There was a major AIDS conference scheduled for the third week of July, which would give the potential buyers of the shares a better view of Retrovir's potential. A sale just before the conference would make the institutions fearful of bad news to come, and thus affect the price they would pay. In the event, it was decided that Wellcome wouldn't attend the conference, to avoid giving either too optimistic a view of Retrovir or of being too cautious.

Finally, too long a delay would have invalidated much of the work on the prospectus, since it would have been out of date. Wellcome's August year-end meant its first-half figures (to 28 February) were scheduled for release on 26 March, but these would only be considered "current" until the end of August. The US election was due in November, and Hillary Clinton, running alongside her husband, was promising to squeeze the drugs companies should he be elected.

Extraordinary as it may seem, all these constraints about the date meant that there was only one weekend during which pricing and allocating the offer was practicable if the sale proceeds were to be maximised. There was a further problem with the state of the stock market. Britain was in the grip of a monetary squeeze, as the Major administration imposed high interest rates to try and keep the pound inside the limits set by the Exchange Rate Mechanism. Companies, home-owners and share prices were all suffering as a result of this policy. It was hardly a good advertisement for US funds considering whether to make a substantial investment in a British company, however international it was in practice.

The size of the offer required a sales technique new to the London market, albeit one familiar to the target US institutions. Rather than have the issue underwritten beforehand – paying the big funds a fee to take any stock that nobody else wanted – Flemings went about "bookbuilding". The potential buyers are invited to indicate how much stock they will take and at what prices, and all the indicative bids are correlated at the last minute.

The trustees had appointed Hambros Bank to reassure them that Flemings' advice and conduct of the deal was pukka. Faced with an interminable, almost impenetrable document, one of the trustees had asked Sir "Chips" Keswick of Hambros if he could distil the essence of the paperwork into a single sentence. "Take £8 a share and run," was Keswick's laconic reply.

The sale was to take place over the weekend of 25 July. On Friday 24 July, James Baker, the US Secretary of State, threatened Saddam Hussein with military action if he did not allow the United Nations' nuclear inspectors into Iraq. Stock markets fell sharply. Gibbs heard the news at lunchtime. He said later, with commendable sang-froid, "There was nothing I could do except to have a jolly good lunch with the inspirational City commentator Christopher Fildes. The Baker announcement was the only fractionally unsettling moment of the six months' exercise." Baker's threat, and the little matter of the Wellcome share price – standing at 20 times prospective 1992 earnings and yielding just 1.7% at a time when interest rates were near double figures – was enough to choke back some of the enthusiasm from US funds.

Nevertheless, the sale went ahead, and on 27 July 1992 the Trust sold 33.5% of the shares at £8 each, a small discount to the then market price. The following day's *Financial Times* described it as "a remarkable success", and might have been thought to answer any concerns the Charity Commissioners may have had. Nevertheless within two weeks of the sale the Chief Charity Commissioner, Richard Fries, wrote to Gibbs with a stinging criticism of the Wellcome sale – the price was much lower than expected, the amount of shares sold was smaller and the fees much larger. Looking back, the timing of the 1992 sale was perfect, laying the foundations for the Trust's enormous financial growth in the following seven years. Through the whole of the 1990s the Trust's assets increased by an average of £1 billion a year. The Trust's holding in Wellcome shares fell from 73.1% to 39.6%, raising £2.3 billion, nearly 12 times the price fetched by the sale of the first 25%. An asset yielding 1.7% was sold, and the proceeds could be reinvested in the world's stock markets where the average yield was almost 5%. The FTSE 100 index, for example, was 2300 at the time. The income of the Trust was more than doubled, and the risk dramatically reduced, with the Wellcome holding down to 26.5 % of the Trust's assets.

The timing was extraordinarily fortunate. While a growing number of commentators had said that sterling's membership of the ERM was unsustainable, predicting just when the façade would crack was impossible. The Deutschemark, the yardstick for the mechanism, was strong against the dollar, which obliged the Bank of England to keep buying sterling at around $2 to the pound, a rate which was patently too high. When Italy's central bank gave up the unequal struggle with the lira, the pressure was instantly transferred to sterling.

Shares had fallen, reflecting the currency crisis, but by the middle of September and after lengthy discussions between John Govett of Schroder and Roger Gibbs, 93% of the £2.3 billion raised from the sale had been reinvested. When the pound finally cracked, on Black Wednesday, 16 September 1992, share prices took off. "Everything we'd invested in for the long term went up by at least 20%, virtually overnight, so it was a wonderful switch," said Gibbs, "so I think I can say, with hindsight, well done Alistair Frame for not pushing his non-executive directors a year earlier. It meant we could get our timing spot on."

As if to reinforce the impression of divine guidance, Clinton won the election, and his wife was put in charge of health care. She talked tough about reforming the drugs companies, and throughout 1993 pharmaceutical stocks were under the cosh. By the middle of 1994 the Wellcome price was well below the £8 achieved in the second offer. At its very worst, the price hit £4.90. As Banks recalled: "Anyway, we did it, and the price fell, and that didn't matter. We didn't get sued, the Company's profits came through pretty well as expected, but increasingly one was beginning to become concerned about something we'd worried about earlier, the Company's pipeline of new drugs – or rather, the lack of one."

It was clear to most observers that another round of consolidation was going to take place. Drugs were, and are, a global industry, but at the time no one company had a market share of more than 4%. The popular image of pharmaceutical research, of slightly eccentric men in white coats stumbling upon unexpected results of their experiment's seemed years out of date, even if it had ever really been true. It still happens, as the history of Viagra showed. Originally developed to combat hypertension, it was only when men in the trials proved reluctant to return their excess pills that Pfizer realised they might have quite another use for it.

The logic of increasing consolidation seemed indisputable. Developing commercial compounds needs increasing scale and financial firepower, patents are progressively harder to establish and more expensive to protect, and governments everywhere question the size of the drugs bill. The response from the drug companies was to build world-wide distribution networks in order to fully exploit the limited window between commercial clearance and patent expiry. Wellcome, it seemed, would either have to make its own acquisitions, or become a target.

Flemings' analysis was clear: Wellcome needed to prepare for change. The bankers argued that it needed to have leadership positions in four, five or six of the major categories of therapeutic medicines to have a secure long-term future. Put this starkly, the trustees were convinced, and quickly realised, once again, that the *status quo* was dangerous if the Trust was to maintain its ability to fund significant research. They suggested Flemings share the analysis with the Company. Says Banks: "We drew up a whole series of tables and presentations. The board listened politely and went away. We never heard from them."

In fact, Pfizer had approached Gibbs verbally in the early 1990s suggesting a deal. He reported the conversation to Robb, but nothing more came of it. Since most of the major drugs houses talk to each other, at various levels, all the time, it would be surprising if the subject had never come up.

The silence from the board rang alarm bells among the trustees, especially as Flemings pointed out the possibility of the opposite problem to the one that had led to the share sales in the first place. If it became apparent to the financial markets that Wellcome's pipeline was running dry, not only would the potential partners disappear, but the share rating would start to suffer. There were distant echoes, once again, of the fate of the Nuffield Foundation.

There was another worrying echo, too. Frame's health had deteriorated to the point where the trustees reckoned that he could not be expected to take the chair at the November 1994 annual meeting. Gibbs with great reluctance advised him to retire. He died at the end of December. There was no obvious successor among the non-executives, and the Trust did not press for an outsider, an error which was to cause further schism between the Trust and Company. The result was that Robb stepped up to executive chairman, a position of power uncomfortably like that enjoyed by Shepperd in 1985. The history of chief executives of big companies stepping up to chairman is not, on the whole, a happy one.

Shortly before Christmas 1994, John Manser and Bernard Taylor, colleagues of Banks, had dinner with Richard Sykes, the chief executive of Glaxo. At the end of the dinner, Sykes asked about the Wellcome Trust.

Bernard pricked up his ears and said: 'Why do you want to know? Lawrence Banks knows them very well.' He didn't answer the question, but called Bernard several days later and said: "I've formed the view that there is an absolutely logical merger between Wellcome plc and Glaxo. They have complementary product lines, sales forces, etc. The whole thing is an absolute natural for Glaxo, Wellcome and for the pharmaceutical industry in the UK."

This can hardly have come as a complete surprise to the Flemings team, given their analysis of the industry. There were only four British drugs companies of any size Glaxo, Wellcome, Beecham and the division of ICI which eventually became Astra Zeneca. They hardly needed Sykes to point out the limited options to Wellcome, once the principle of greater size was accepted.

Earlier in 1994, Banks had had a personal meeting with Robb at which Banks had warned him about over-reliance on the memorandum of understanding he had extracted from the trustees two years before. "I told him that someone may come along and make an offer for the Company, and I think it is a possibility that it will happen over the next two years." The trustees had been legally advised that their fiduciary duty would over-ride any number of memoranda. "I said to him: 'However much I like you or respect what you have done for the Company, ultimately there's going to be a cold-blooded calculation as to whether the Trust would be better off selling or not selling.'

Flemings' own position was hardly altruistic, either. Investment banks make money in all sorts of ways, but the big paydays come with big deals, and advising the target company in a multi-billion pound takeover is about as big as deals get. Its analysis that the future lay with the big battalions was honest and sincere, but it happily coincided with the bank's own self-interest.

Gibbs was advised that if he got a telephone call from Sykes he should take it seriously. It didn't take long. On 20 December 1994, Sykes contacted Gibbs and suggested lunch early in the New Year. Nothing more was said and the lunch took place on 10 January 1995. Gibbs had never met any of the Glaxo directors, except one non-executive, Lord Kingsdown, who as Robin Leigh-Pemberton had been Governor of the Bank of England when Gibbs was at the top of his trade in the money markets. "I had had lunch or meetings with a wide variety of chief executives of large pharmaceutical companies around the world over the previous three or four years, notably Pfizers, so this was not necessarily anything significant."

Gibbs said: "At the lunch I said to Richard Sykes exactly what I said to everyone else: 'We are now 60% diversified, we've been used to having over 95% of our eggs in one basket, we now only have 40% in that basket, and we're very happy about the management. We don't wish to do anything.' We had an agreement with the Company that we would not make any approach to any other pharmaceutical company for at least five years from summer 1992, and we didn't. We'd also tried hard to stop any company building up a 10% stake."

Says Gibbs: "At the lunch we had a most interesting discussion about the pharmaceutical world, and I mean all over the world, and how it might end up in a few years' time. Richard Sykes said: 'I would think it will be five or six big companies in five years' time. When leaving the lunch Sykes said quietly to Gibbs. "So you are happy with your Wellcome shareholding – but you do have your fiduciary duties." Gibbs readily agreed.

It did not take Sykes long to react. Two days later, his advisers Lazards were in informal contact with Flemings, having those entirely hypothetical, but immensely practical, conversations that so often precede takeover deals. Had the conversations been anything other than entirely hypothetical, formal statements would have had to be made to the Stock Exchange, raising the possibility of the deal being aborted. Banks recalls being asked the theoretical question by Lazards and Sykes: "On what basis might you recommend an offer to the trustees?"

The Trustees had asked themselves the same question. Gibbs recalls thinking that even at the current £6.80 the share price had got ahead of events. "We would have expected, at best in five years' time, a share price of £8. We were very worried that Wellcome might be beginning to run out of steam. But we did not initiate the Glaxo bid in any shape or form. Going public in 1986 was a calculated decision by David Steel. The share sale in 1992 was a calculated decision. The Glaxo bid was thrust on us."

At lunch with Banks's colleague Bernard Taylor, Sykes suggested £8 a share, a healthy premium to the then market price of around £6.80, but hardly an offer the trustees couldn't refuse. By the end of the hypothetical discussions, Glaxo was talking about somewhere above £10. "We said: 'Well, if you were to make such an offer we think it is highly likely that we would recommend it to the trustees."

Glaxo's shares were also attractive. Gibbs said: "The opportunity of taking 30% of a highly-priced bid in Glaxo shares was too good to miss. Even

I could see that on a yield of 6.4% they were very cheap."

The signal from Banks was the green light Sykes was seeking, and on Friday 20 January Glaxo wrote to the Trust with a knockout takeover offer. At £10.25 a share in a mixture of cash and Glaxo shares: it would value Wellcome at £9.1 billion. It was irresistible from a financial viewpoint, but it came with two painful conditions: the Trust had to sign an irrevocable agreement to sell its holding to Glaxo, and that the Trust would not contact the Company before the bid was launched.

That weekend the trustees had to make a tough decision. The offer was clearly highly attractive. Even at £6.80, the Wellcome price already had some takeover froth in it, as others had identified it as a possible bid target. The trustees also knew that the twin drivers of the Company's profits, Zovirax and Retrovir, were peaking. The 1995 sales figures confirmed their suspicions; Zovirax sales were flat. Retrovir was actually down by 12%, as AIDS confounded the pessimists who had predicted an epidemic in the west.

Glaxo's price was unlikely to be beaten by any among the very small group of possible buyers. None could realistically find £10 billion in cash, and an offer which was mostly in shares would present the trustees with a new problem, of a holding which was too big to sell but too small to represent effective control. Furthermore, an offer of shares in a non-UK company would have left the Trustees with an indigestible lump of stock in a market none of them knew much about.

The risk of a leak, or of Glaxo launching a bid without the trustees' agreement, perhaps at a lower price, was very real. In either case, the trustees would find themselves thrown on the defensive. Yet the memorandum of understanding could not be ignored altogether, and to agree to Glaxo's terms would drive straight through it, both in accepting the bid and in not informing the Company first.

The trustees pointed out that they could not agree to ignore a higher bid from elsewhere, however unlikely it was, and the Glaxo camp accepted the point. By late Sunday evening, the trustees had decided to accept the offer terms, and £10.25 per Wellcome share, 70% in cash and 30% in Glaxo shares. They braced themselves for a hostile reaction from the Company.

First thing on Monday 23 January, Gibbs and Cazalet went to Wellcome's Euston head office to break the bad news personally to John Robb before the market opened. Gibbs recalls that Robb's car had failed to start that morning, so he had used his wife's, which had no mobile phone in it (the hand-held models in 1995 were more suitable for weight-lifters). He finally got to the office at 8.15, half an hour after the trustees.

Robb was stunned at this bolt from the blue. However much he might have been warned about the Trust's fiduciary duty, it's clear he was totally unprepared for the moment his horse was shot from under him. Although the Trust's holding did not add up to legal control, it would have been practically impossible for another company to win a bid contest with their stake pledged to another buyer.

Robb's position was further weakened by the market's reaction to the bid, which was to mark up Glaxo's share price, making the offer worth still more. The first reaction by the market-makers and short-term share traders to a complex deal is more visceral than logical, but it is uncanny how many times the first move of the share price, either up or down, is a good indicator of whether a deal adds long-term value to the acquirer or not. By the time the bid closed in March, it was worth £10.60 per Wellcome share. Shortly after, the value went to £11. The market had effectively given the takeover the seal of approval.

The Company launched a legal action to try and enforce the memorandum, but the board was quickly forced to accept that the trustees had sold out that first weekend. The only real uncertainty was whether another bidder would emerge, offering an even higher price. In that event, the trustees had to be free to accept it – again, it was a matter of fiduciary duty to maximise the proceeds from the sale of their prime asset. It was clear that Wellcome's days of independence were over, and that one of an incumbent management's principal weapons, the almost ritual rejection of an approach on the grounds that it undervalued the business, had been spiked by the Trustees' acceptance of Glaxo's terms. Yet this did not seem to be immediately clear to Robb and his colleagues. As Banks explained later: "What he ought to have said was 'I'm amazed that the Trust should have done this without consulting me. However, Glaxo is a marvellous company and we're perfectly prepared to work at discussions. We have a duty to see whether we can find any other buyers. We can't take the unilateral view that there is nobody else out there who might bid.'

That would have been a perfectly sensible reaction and would have led on to discussions with Glaxo. Robb would, I think, have become non-executive deputy chairman of Glaxo-Wellcome and the whole thing would have proceeded on that basis.

There was plenty of speculation about the possibility of a counter-bid.

After all, this was an opportunity that was not going to recur, the chance for a "strategic acquisition", a phrase which is usually code for explaining why a buyer has paid too much. The two names in the frame were Roche and Zeneca. No counter-bidder would have had a chance without first securing a similar agreement from the trustees, who waited. Roche never knocked on the door, and as for Zeneca, it was keen but chaotic. It demanded an undertaking that the Trust accept no other offers, even higher ones, but never quite said how much it was prepared to pay. Looking back the Zeneca offer was never likely to be acceptable.

There was much bad blood as it became clear to Robb that his independence was lost. He had his own plans to grow by acquisition, but had not shared such strategic thoughts with the largest shareholder. He argued that the price was too low, and that others would be prepared to pay more, if only they were given enough time to organise a counter-bid. Yet as Gibbs said later: "What's really remarkable is that during the entire process of seven weeks between the launch of the Glaxo bid and it becoming unconditional, not one person from any pharmaceutical company throughout the world made any contact with me."

Robb's feeling of frustration is understandable. He was doing a perfectly competent job, and his belief that the business was protected from a predator by a big, friendly shareholder was obviously a useful asset when trying to persuade good people to come and work at Wellcome rather than elsewhere. He could point to the memorandum with its undertaking not to solicit takeover approaches, nor to sell more shares without first consulting the Company.

It is not impossible that, given more time, he might have found a buyer prepared to top the Glaxo bid. With less confrontational tactics, he might have coaxed another few pennies per share from Sykes in return for agreement, since agreed deals ensure the co-operation of the management, allowing the integration of businesses to proceed more smoothly.

Yet as a Euromoney Books study called *The Art of the Deal* by Robert Lilja concludes: "While it was John Robb's duty, as the chairman of Wellcome plc, to procure the best possible offer for all his shareholders, he is not justified in attacking the Trust. First, the 1992 memorandum was not legally binding. Second, neither the memorandum nor the Deed of Covenant could result in the trustees having to do, or omit to do, anything which they considered contrary to the best interests of the Trust. This language is clearly included in the 1992 prospectus."

So the Company knew, or should have known, all along that it could not rely on the memorandum to be a permanent shield against a takeover. A far better strategy would have been to treat the Trust as the owners they had once been, rather than simply as another name on the share register. There is a qualitative, as well as a quantitative difference between being a 40% and a 4% shareholder. This should have been apparent to the board all along, and if they needed a lesson, they only had to look back at the breakdown in communications in their own company that led to the flotation in the first place.

The annual reports of the Wellcome Trust make its twin objectives quite plain: to advance medical research and to support museums and libraries for the study of sciences allied to medicine. As the reports do not need to add, everything else is detail.

One detail that becomes apparent from the documents is the brilliance of the investment strategies the trustees have pursued. The proceeds of the three sales of the holdings in Wellcome plc have been invested widely. By 1995, the Wellcome Trust had become the largest charitable organisation in the world, prompting the Ford Foundation to amend its writing paper from "the largest charitable foundation in the world" to "one of the largest charitable foundations in the world".

When Gibbs retired as chairman of the Trust in December 1999, the assets had passed £14 billion. Its holding in Glaxo Wellcome, 4½ % of that company's equity, was worth just under £2½ billion. It is impossible to say what Wellcome would have been worth on its own at that date, had the Trust retained 100%, but it's safe to say that it would have been nowhere near £14 billion. Nor would the Trust have been able to fund so much valuable and extraordinary research from dividends received.

Looking back, it's clear that Flemings' analysis of where the industry was going was open to question, although it was quite correct in forecasting a wave of mergers. The industry had been expected to grow at more than 4% a year indefinitely and however plausible the projections seemed, trees do not grow up to the sky. In his judgment in 1992, Lord Hoffman had not seriously expected the Wellcome Trust to end up owning the whole world. In 1995, the Wellcome takeover turned Glaxo into the country's most valuable company. By the turn of the century, Glaxo Wellcome itself was merging again, to form GlaxoSmithKline.

Yet the glittering prospects that such mega-mergers were supposed to bring were an illusion. Pharmaceutical shares have been progressively de-rated as it became clear that size alone was not enough to generate major new drugs. This is an industry-wide problem; Pfizer's market value in late 2008 was much less than it had paid to take over Warner Lambert and Pharmacia. As Professor Mahmud Hassan of Rutgers University concluded: "Despite the attractiveness of mergers in the pharmaceutical industry, we find no abnormal returns from mergers for acquiring companies."

The pace of discovery of major new drugs has fallen dramatically, despite the billions spent looking. In retrospect, there was a golden age of medical breakthroughs in the 1970s and 1980s. It seemed only a matter of time before the researchers would be making serious inroads into the remaining big killers, especially after the unpicking of gene sequences offered the tantalising prospect of understanding diseases at the molecular level. During Wellcome's brief life as a public company, the pharmaceutical sector was highly rated by the market.

Yet finding cures for cancers or Alzheimer's is proving a painfully slow process, and it's one where size doesn't seem to help. On his arrival in 2008, the new chief executive of GlaxoSmithKline immediately broke up its laboratories into smaller units in an attempt to mimic the entrepreneurial flair that big companies so often lack. The big deals, it seems now, merely distracted the senior management from the research. Perhaps the image of the slightly nutty professor doing strange things in his lab, pursuing some crackpot theory of his own, is not as far away from the optimum research process after all.

Fortunately for the beneficiaries of the Wellcome Trust, the fate of the commercial pharmaceutical industry is no longer of direct concern to their benefactor. In his chairman's statement, written in December 2007, Sir William Castell could claim that since the flotation of the Wellcome Foundation Limited to become Wellcome plc in 1986, the Trust's portfolio had grown at a compound rate of 16.2%. He added: "It remains well diversified with over 600 funds and managers. The net value of the Trust's asset base was £15.1 billion at 30 September 2007."

The portfolio has been radically restructured over the years, with sales of British equities balanced by investments into hedge funds, residential property, emerging markets and medical venture capital. British shares account for less than 15% of the total assets, and the Trust has no direct holding in the massive combine of which Wellcome plc is a relatively small part. Henry Wellcome would undoubtedly be surprised to find what has happened to his legacy, but he would surely be delighted at what the Trust has become today.

CHAPTER 12

The Wellcome Trust Today

This book was conceived as a memoir of my experience at the Wellcome Trust up to my retirement in 1991.

I thought, as did the publisher Jeremy Greenwood, that it would be useful if we could bring the story up to the present by a chapter about The Trust today. This chapter would have to be written by the Trust itself since my only knowledge of this period was in its publications. The Trust decided that as the book was my memoir a large chapter such as would be necessary to give a fair description of the Trust today would unbalance the narrative and that they wished to leave the chapter to me to compose. In retrospect one could see that no one could write it in the style of a memoir because during the 18 years, that have elapsed, there have been three chairmen and three directors and such enormous growth that it will take a devoted historian to cover this period. Fortunately the facts can be retrieved from the annual reports of the Trust and the extensive information available on the internet.

The central point is that during this period the Trust's capital rose to £15 billion and the income available for expenditure on the objectives set out in Sir Henry Wellcome's will to £600million in 2009. To describe how this sum was used will also be a gargantuan task and outside the purpose of this book. As an interested observer one can only guess the influence of such a large annual injection into the world of medical research. There can be very few research workers or institutions in Britain that have not received support in some form at some stage.

The basis of this enormous increase in size and activity was what happened up to 2000 and so it is necessary to see what had to be launched after that time in order to use the new funds. The first structure that had to be created was a division to handle the investment and management of the funds that were now the Trust's responsibility. This organisation had been born with the first sale of Wellcome shares in 1986 but now was on a much larger scale. Today it is responsible for the core fund of about £15 billion. The expansion of financial affairs meant more staff and these had to be accommodated. Park Square West was far too small and so a major reconstruction of the Wellcome Building was undertaken during my last years. The Trust moved in shortly after I retired and the whole building accommodated not only the grants and financial offices but also the Medical Historical Library and a new museum called Science for Life which recognised the need for the Trust to reach out to the public to describe what it was for.

The greatly increased funds made it possible for the Trust to take on major capital projects and to commit funds for their future. Such an example was The Wellcome Sanger Institute at Hinxton near Cambridge which was established to read the human genome. Plans have been announced for a new Institute for Medical Research in London which will bring together the Medical Research Council, the Cancer funds and University College. Many other laboratories in universities all over the country have been built and funds provided for their programmes of research. The laboratories in Kenya and South East Asia have been expanded and funded. A major collaboration with India was announced in the Trust's latest annual report. The Trust plays a major role in developing stem cell research.

In addition, the seedbed of research, the universities, have been given support of every type, major equipment, scholarships, fellowships and long term appointments.

Major epidemiological studies are underway to discover the effect of genes on health. Links have been made with the arts and the history of medicine activity has expanded.

To process all this activity more staff were needed and so more accommodation. A completely new office was built, the Gibbs Building. The Wellcome Building was used to create a new exhibition called the Wellcome Collection, which has proved very popular.

For all this to happen and be managed a completely new structure had to be created. Wellcome Trustees became Governors with a wider range of experience. No longer was it possible to have the personal interface with the research workers that provided such a stimulus to the medical and scientific staff of the early years. The Trust today is a completely different place from the one that I have described in this book. It is able to do immensely more for the research community but it has inevitably lost the personal fairy godmother role which was so important for building its reputation and provided such a wonderful life for those who worked in it.

Valete

It has not always been straightforward and obvious how the Wellcome Trust should develop. From time to time it had been necessary to take drastic action to keep it on the road. Sometimes good fortune intervened to its advantage at others the clash of cultures between scientific discovery and the business world raised controversial problems which had to be resolved.

Its early years under the founders of the Company exemplified the imaginative development of a business enterprise and the way in which a company can decay when its leader directs his interests elsewhere while continuing to exert influence. Later when pioneering the introduction of laboratories into the pharmaceutical industry Wellcome was persuaded that they would not recruit top class scientists if they did not have independence. The Wellcome Laboratories produced many Fellows of the Royal Society but few blockbuster products for sale. On the other hand the American branch showed how the development of basic research with a slant towards a marketable product could be immensely successful and profitable and also win two Nobel Prizes as well. This contrast brought out the difficult overlap when the company management does not have a sufficient understanding of research. This difficulty is especially highlighted when the owners' experience is in the support of academic science, and with little understanding of the industrial environment. In the case of the Wellcome trustees this situation could not be easily resolved if they were to avoid interference in the Company and overstep the position of shareholders. As trustees of a charity there were restrictions against owning a profitable enterprise particularly, for the Trust, one in the pharmaceutical industry. During the Franks era the separation was particularly great. By the time Steel took over other forces had come to bear as a result of the success of the company and the danger of having all one's eggs in one basket. The only possible solution was to sell shares and therefore divorce the Trust from the activities of the Company.

During my time the Trust moved from being a bit part player in the world of medical research to being one of the largest private supporters of the field. I revolved in the company of happy colleagues and friends in the world of great scientists with innovative ideas. During my last year, my school in Trinidad decided to hold an Open Day in the science laboratories and I arranged exhibitions of the evolution of plants and animals. I was fascinated by the wide variety of forms, intriguing mechanisms and the interactions between both branches of the kingdom of nature. Who would have thought that I could have made a career with the people at the forefront of discovery in these fields. Learning the skills to become a physician was a very important preparation but I never regretted putting them on one side to become a philanthropoid, the word I coined to describe the role of a person who gives away a philanthropist's money. I wonder if Aristotle would agree with the way we solved his problem!

Appendices

The Development of the Trust's offices and the Wellcome Building (1958-91)

When I joined the Wellcome Trust it was housed at 52 Queen Anne Street which crosses Harley and Wimpole Streets and is two blocks from the Royal Society of Medicine. It was an attractive building with a rather charming front door, which Frank Green had painted bright red. It had a basement in which the caretaker, Mrs Abrahart, lived.

The ground floor had a waiting room on the left which Maurice Barren, the Trust's first Administrative Officer, subsequently occupied, and a fairly large room at the back which was the general office in which there were Dr Green's secretary and a young woman of about 18 who was her assistant and took a bit of shorthand and dealt with the switchboard.

There was no duplicating equipment in the office so Frank Green's secretary typed out all the trustees' papers twice with carbons. The bottom copy, which I received, was pretty illegible. One of my early introductions was a cyclostyle – in which waxed paper is used to form a template for printing on a rotating drum machine – a pretty mucky procedure with black printers ink all over someone's hands. Later on, during Lord Piercy's time, we acquired a copying machine, using a wet process, which meant that all the copies had to be hung up to dry on clothes-pegs around the room.

The floor above the front office was occupied by Frank Green and the large room at the back by Dale. Above there were two small rooms in the front occupied respectively by Dale's secretary and Colonel Bensted, who came into the office part-time to help Frank, mainly with the travel grants. The larger room at the back became my office, and above that there was an attractive flat that had been let out privately. Later my back room was divided and I moved into Dale's office and Edda Hanington into Frank Green's, occupied in between by Boyd,). The basement that had been vacated by the caretaker was converted into offices and a little later we broke through into the basement next door to have even more accommodation.

The search for new premises and Park Square West

It had become obvious by 1970 that the Trust had out-grown Queen Anne Street and so I set Maurice Barren onto the task of searching for a new office. One day, he told me of the availability of a block on Ulster Place, together with No 1 Park Square West, Regent's Park which was available for rebuilding on a 99-year Crown Estates lease. I had always hankered for a building on the Park and immediately became enthusiastic. I visited the building which was very run-down with temporary offices and rather sleazy bed-sitting rooms built around a number of up and down narrow houses.

We obtained permission to keep 1 Park Square West in its original shape but with considerable refurbishment, and join it into a new building which was erected behind the original façade of Ulster Place which fronted on to the Euston Rd at the top end of Harley Street. The Camden Council insisted on our keeping the original front wall, which, incidentally, had no foundations. So very elaborate scaffolding was built and the building behind was completely gutted. A new steel structured building was then erected to fit with the front walls and provide four floors and a basement with a large garage.

This building was obviously much larger than the Trust required at that time and so we rented out the top floor to the Postgraduate Medical Federation and two of the flats to private tenants. When we first moved into the office we really rattled but it was a very wise move because, with the growth of the Trust, not only did we need our own floors but had to ask the Postgraduate Medical Federation to leave. And later on the flats also were incorporated as temporary offices.

It was always an extremely pleasant building to have developed because it looked so good. We had a pen and ink drawing done of it soon after we moved. The cost of the building, including carpeting and furnishing, was about £800,000.

The Wellcome Building

My first experience of the Wellcome Building was when I was a medical student. I used the Museum of Medical Science to learn some tropical medicine for my finals and higher qualifications. I found it immensely valuable.

In 1948 I decided to edit a book , *Careers in Medicine*. I was seeking a publisher for this book and it was suggested to me that I should go to see Poynter. I well remember that meeting. I was taken up to the Hall of Statuary which was full of book stacks. Poynter had a desk at the top of the stairs and he met me overlooking this mass of old books that then comprised the face of the library, the rest of it being in store elsewhere. At that time I had no idea that my future would be so strongly linked with this building. Also at that time, the galleries near the entrance served as an exhibition area for some of the medical historical artefacts in the Wellcome collection. It was later that Dr Underwood developed the pharmacies that became such a feature of the building.

My next visit to the building was when I was interviewed in John Boyd's laboratory for the post of Assistant Scientific Secretary of the Trust.

The Wellcome Building had been built by Henry Wellcome to house his Museum and Library and the laboratories of the Wellcome Bureau of Scientific Research. It belonged to the Company and had become its headquarters. I have written elsewhere of the transfer of the historical collections to the Trust and the destruction of the laboratories to make way for the expansion of the business into the area occupied by them. Not only had the Company expanded, but so also had the Library and Museum so that, at its zenith, the History of Medicine Exhibition occupied the whole of the first floor, the Library the second floor and quite a lot of the third. When the transfer of the Museum collection to the Science Museum took place, the exhibition was dismantled and the Chairman of the Company's suite occupied a third of the Museum area. This uneasy relationship swayed back and forth over many years as the Company recognised that it needed a larger and more convenient headquarters building.

This uncertainty led me to wonder what we would do if one day we found ourselves unable to house the Library in the Wellcome Building. We therefore debated whether it could be housed in the country or had to be somewhere else in London. We thought about amalgamating it into the University but the eventual solution came about one day when I was looking out of my office in the Wellcome Building, and admiring the former Cambridge University Press across the road. Someone said to me: "You know that building is up for sale, it is only temporarily occupied by the National Union of Railwaymen and they will wish to sell it." The trustees agreed to buy and be prepared to move the Library into that building.

Eventually the Company decided not to develop the Wellcome Building. Nevertheless, we had acquired Bentley House and decided to make it the main repository for the Library in the future. The Wellcome Company eventually moved out and the Trust purchased the Wellcome Building at the time of the flotation. The Trust therefore then had available both the Wellcome Building and Bentley House and we joined them by a tunnel under the Euston Road – an interesting exercise!

The Wellcome Building Development

Wellcome plc moved out of the Wellcome Building at the end of 1989: they had occupied it for 48 years. The Trust had begun to outgrow its accommodation in Park Square West and before long it had to house people in various offices in the neighbourhood. It was fairly obvious that we would have to move somewhere and there was the Wellcome Building which we owned, together with Bentley House across the road. It seemed only sensible to refashion Henry Wellcome's original creation to house all of the activities of the Trust, its historical library and its offices. The outcome would have given him enormous pleasure.

It was a very large building and at that time we thought that there would be an enormous amount of space that we could not fill. We had ideas for offering accommodation to other charities that support medical research, and learned societies. The concept developed that the building could become a national centre and indeed a focal point for medical research that would not only provide meeting rooms and a lecture theatre but, also, an information resource and a public exhibition about developments in medical research and how they came about. We set about the plan with enthusiasm and over the next few years developed an exhibition to be called the Science for Life, an information resources centre, and separate meeting rooms. It gradually became obvious that there would be no accommodation available for outsiders as the Trust grew and grew to keep pace with the increasing income. After I retired a completely new office, The Gibbs Building, was erected. It adjoins the Wellcome Building and was created from the property owned by the National Union of Railwaymen as well as the MI6 building. Now the whole site is precisely the same as the original one bought by Henry Wellcome in the 1930s.

Science for Life exhibition

The idea was to create an exhibition that would attempt to inform the public about medical research and remove the image of the poor sick child and faceless boffins that was so popular for fund raising. Laurence Smaje, Bridget Ogilvie, Steve Emberton, and I met fortnightly to develop the various themes of the exhibition of which the major one was a "walk-in" cell. The idea for this had come from Billie (my wife) and it did seem to be an excellent way to convey the central point that cell biology had come to occupy in the world of medical research.

The building that was supposed to be completed in October 1991 was still a long way from being finished at Easter 1992. It was decided to terminate the contract with the builders and take on another contractor to bring the building to completion. The Trust moved to the Wellcome Building in 1992 after I had retired.

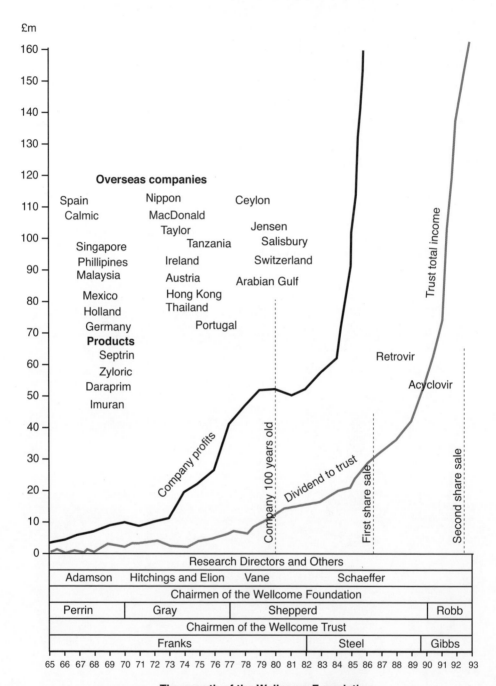

The growth of the Wellcome Foundation

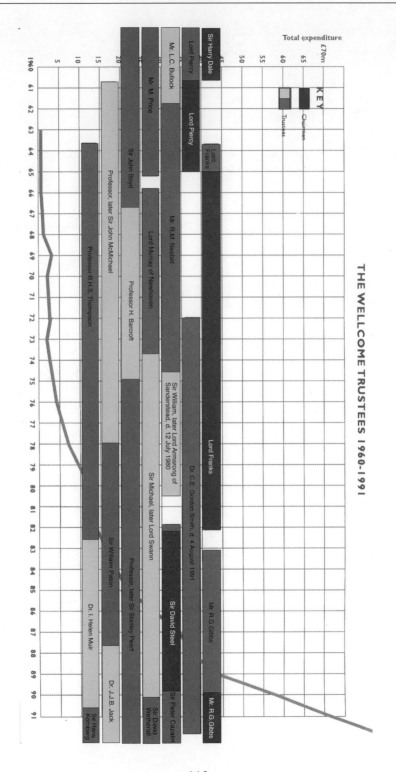

THE WELLCOME TRUSTEES 1960-1991

113

Sources

Books

In Pursuit of Excellence 1880-1980, 1980 by Wellcome Foundation at its Centenary

Physic and Philanthropy by A.R. Hall and B.A.Bembridge 1986 Cambridge University Press

Henry Dale -Thesis for PhD by E H Tansey 1990

Personal Recollections by Peter Williams 1992

Oliver Franks Founding Father by Alex Danchev 1993 Clarendon Press, Oxford

Wellcome Institute for the History of Medicine –A short History by John Symons 1993

Henry Wellcome by Robert Rhodes James 1994 Hodder and Stoughton

The Wellcome Trust Illustrated History of Tropical Diseases. Edited by C E G Cox 1996 Wellcome Trust

Wellcome's Legacies, Sir Henry Wellcome and Tropical Medicine by L.G.Goodwin and E.Beveridge and *The Development of Chemical Research in the Wellcome Laboratories UK 1896-1965* by J.H.Gorvin 1998

The Exotic Fruits of my Life by Peter Williams 2003 Rana

Burroughs Wellcome and Co. 1880-1940 by Roy Childs and E.M. Tansey 2007 Crucible Books

Interviews of people concerned with the history of the Trust

Trustees

Lord Franks of Headington	1991
Sir David Steel and Sir Roger Gibbs	1996
Sir Stanley Peart	1996
Dr. Helen Muir	1996

114

Sir Peter Cazalet   1996

Wellcome Foundation Limited

Sir Alfred Shepperd	1996
Dr. Len Goodwin	1996
Dr. James Howard	1996
Dr. Gertrude Elion	1997
Dr. Howard Schaeffer	1997

Trust Staff and Advisers

Dr. Peter Williams	1995
Dr. Peter Williams	1996
Dr. Edda Hanington	1996
Mr Ian Macgregor	1996
Professor AR Hall	1997
Dr. David Gordon	1999
Mr Francis Tufton and Mr Richard Hodges	1996
Mr. Russell Denoon Duncan	1996
Mr Lawrence Banks	1996

Other sources

Round table discussion, Burroughs Wellcome Fund
Reports of the Trust from 1936-91
Talks given in different places during my work with the Trust bound with the contemporary policy introductions in Trust reports.
Articles published in connection with the Trust in relation to universities, other private funds, tropical medicine etc.

116